I0110820

THE RADICAL DISCIPLE

THE RADICAL DISCIPLE

Three Pamphlets Inspired
by Koinonia Partners

Bill Lane Doulos

FOREWORD BY
Ched Myers

CASCADE *Books* • Eugene, Oregon

THE RADICAL DISCIPLE
Three Pamphlets Inspired by Koinonia Partners

Copyright © 2015 Koinonia Farm. All rights reserved. Except for brief
quotations in critical publications or reviews, no part of this book may
be reproduced in any manner without prior written permission from the
publisher. Write: Permissions. Wipf and Stock Publishers, 199 W. 8th Ave.,
Suite 3, Eugene, OR 97401.

Cascade Books
An Imprint of Wipf and Stock Publishers
199 W. 8th Ave., Suite 3
Eugene, OR 97401

www.wipfandstock.com

ISBN 13: 978-1-62564-868-6

Cataloguing-in-Publication Data

Doulos, Bill Lane.

The radical disciple : three pamphlets inspired by Koinonia Partners / Bill
Lane Doulos.

x + 80 p. ; 23 cm.

ISBN 13: 978-1-62564-868-6

1. Christianity and culture. 2. Social change—Religious aspects—Christianity. 3. Anabaptists. I. Title.

BR148 .D69 2015

Manufactured in the U.S.A.   01/21/2016

CONTENTS

FOREWORD

By Ched Myers

"RADICALISM HAS ALWAYS BEEN part of the fabric of Christian theology and life," writes Christopher Rowland. The foremost interpreter of the long, if perpetually marginalized, history of radical Christianity (see Rowland, 1988), he identifies the "common ingredients" among diverse movements throughout the centuries as "a critique of false religion [and] a hope for a new world . . . that is to be found on earth." Both passions are reflected in these period essays by Bill Lane Doulos.

Doulos was a child (as I was) of a North American expression of this radical tradition that dates to the middle part of the last century. We both owe a great spiritual debt to a leading light of that movement, the great Baptist farmer and theologian Clarence Jordan. Ladon Sheats, a Jordan disciple, introduced Bill and me separately to Clarence's radical gospel in the 1970s, and our lives were permanently changed.

Doulos, born in 1943, graduated from Westminster College in New Wilmington, Pennsylvania. He met Ladon while he was a staff instructor for Young Life in inner-city Pittsburgh, and subsequently visited Koinonia Farm in Georgia for several summers beginning in 1971. After Bill had completed a Masters of Divinity at Fuller Theological Seminary in 1973, Ladon asked him to compile unpublished material from Clarence. Doulos then spent long hours in the shack where Clarence had done his writing at Koinonia, listening to tapes and records and going through papers.

The result was *Cotton Patch Parables of Liberation* (1976). I am grateful to Wipf & Stock for their commitment to preserve this (and so many other radical Christian writings of this generation, a corpus that now includes pamphlets published at Koinonia, of which the present volume is one).

I asked Bill if he stands by the fiery essays in this book, essays now four decades old. He laughed. On one hand, he admits that (quoting Glen Campbell) "the road to my horizon has been full of compromisin'." On the other hand, he points out that "nothing I wrote is as radical as what Jesus said, so I'm content to let these words stand."

Since penning them, Doulos served on the staff of All Saints Episcopal Church in Pasadena, California, from 1974 to 2002, during which time he was executive director of Union Station Foundation, a soup kitchen and homeless shelter, helped start other nonprofit organizations promoting affordable housing, and published two other books (1989, 1995). In 2002, Bill began the Jubilee Transitional Housing ministry of Church of Our Saviour in San Gabriel, California, working with those in recovery from addiction. Recently, at age seventy, he was ordained a deacon in the Episcopal Church. Doulos has indeed been faithful to his 1970s vision of radical discipleship and solidarity with the marginalized.

The first essay herein is an extended meditation on Clarence's assertion that "faith is living in scorn of consequences." The second reflects on servanthood, community, and celebration as marks of the true church. The third and longest essay addresses the "monstrosity" of Christian affluence by mustering every biblical argument Doulos could think of to counter the materially contented church. Superficially, these pieces may seem somewhat dated; but at a deeper level, they represent a continuation of the ancient argument that prophetic faith has always had with religious establishments, which goes back to the beginnings of Scripture itself.

Authentic attempts to recover and recontextualize the Word for the world—which Clarence, Koinonia, and Doulos all dared to do—renew the life of the church, however much it may resist and resent them. Forty years ago these essays reflected the yearning of a new generation of disillusioned yet energized evangelicals for the whole gospel for the whole world. I pray they will resonate with the current rising movement of emergent, missional, and new monastic believers, that they may in turn bear this gospel to the next generation. For such is the genealogy of radical faith.

References

Doulos, Bill Lane. *A Journey of Compassion: Letters from a Street Minister.* South Pasadena, CA: Lizardi Communications, 1989.

Doulos, Bill Lane. *Hearts on Fire: The Evolution of an Urban Church.* Pasadena, CA: The Castle Press, 1995.

Jordan, Clarence, and Bill Lane Doulos. *Cotton Patch Parables of Liberation.* Scottdale, PA: Herald, 1976. (Anniversary ed. 2001.)

Rowland, Christopher. *Radical Christianity*, Oxford, UK: Polity, 1988.

NOTE

The reader should have available a Bible to look up the numerous passages mentioned. They form a necessary part of this writing. Passages quoted are from the Jerusalem Bible (JB) or the Revised Standard Version (RSV), unless otherwise indicated.

I

THE CHRISTIAN RADICAL

1. LIGHT INTO DARKNESS
—A RADICAL CONCEPT

THERE ARE TWO BASIC motivations for being radical. There are those who are radical because they want to accomplish something, and there are those who are radical because they believe something has already been accomplished. These differences in motivation are sometimes only theoretical, but they are also often critical. They may mean the difference between frustration and faithfulness.

I am aware that I have led the reader into a dark forest of unexplained words. I have written that first paragraph with precision, and I hope that my meaning will become clear as I define my terms. And as my meaning becomes clear, I trust that the reader will become capable of both intellectual assent and action response.

Let us examine first of all the term *radical*.

According to Webster, a radical is "one that advocates a decided and often extreme change from existing, usual, or traditional views, habits, conditions, or methods." I can subscribe to that description of myself wholeheartedly, at least in terms of my yearnings, if not in terms of my actions.

The denotation of the word, that is, the strict literal definition, which we find in Webster, is one that should embrace all Christians. The term *radical* conjures up all kinds of images that we must reject (violence, arrogance, etc.), but we cannot be followers of Jesus Christ and reject radicalism per se.

Light coming into darkness is the radical biblical description of Jesus coming into the world. When light confronts darkness, a change is demanded. The change is so complete that it might actually be termed a reversal. The darkness is transformed so that the end result of the bright light of Jesus coming into a sinful world is "an extreme change from existing . . . conditions."

Now it is true that the world has rejected such a change and has crucified Jesus. Crucifixion is the most extreme rejection, just as conversion is fanatic acceptance. The radical onslaught of light is so uncompromising that it demands such an either-or response. The world as a whole has made one response: "He came to his own domain and his own people did not accept him" (John 1:11, JB). But some have made an opposite response just as extreme in its own right as crucifixion: "But to all who did accept him he gave power to become children of God" (John 1:12, JB).

So we have in our own day the same elements of radical confrontation that Jesus experienced in his day. We have no historical or biblical basis for saying that the world has become any more receptive to truth during the twenty centuries since the birth of Jesus. Both history and the Bible point instead to a deterioration process. We Christians are supposed to be and indeed must be the light that is penetrating a dark world. There is a kingdom of God, represented by us, and a kingdom of Satan, represented by the "existing, usual, or traditional views, habits, conditions, or methods."

In the face of this situation, a Christian must be careful to observe two principles.

First of all, no Christian may assume that he is free from internal darkness. We are all struggling against the darkness around us, of course; but we must all recognize that, unlike Jesus, the darkness is also within us. The radical change has begun within us, and a sharp battle is now being waged. We have confidence in the outcome because we have confidence in Jesus. But we must not overlook the fact that we have not yet "arrived" (Phil 3:12, NIV).

Once we understand that reality, we must be even more careful to observe the second principle: we must not bless the status quo. We can readily see the temptation that arises the more we appreciate the forces that are at work within us. We coexist every day with evil. That is a fact that means this life is a great tension for us. But we do not, we must not, we cannot, peacefully coexist with evil. We don't say, "Live and let live." The light and the darkness cannot coexist in peace. The status quo in our lives is that we are sinners; the status quo in the world is darkness. We do not accept either. Even granted that we will always be sinners until the Lord returns, we can't be lulled into apathy. If we lessen the continuing demand for extreme change, we show that we are not children of light, and we no longer represent the radical alternative of the kingdom of God.

We can never make our peace with a world to which Jesus brought a sword, until Jesus returns and "the kingdom of the world has become the kingdom of our Lord and his Christ" (Rev 11:15, RSV).

It is clear that we as Christians cannot accept radicalism for its own sake. For the light of Jesus Christ has a well-defined content. Jesus himself is the content. He represents a "condition" and a "method" that are distinct, and that are clearly presented in the New Testament. So we do not go about simply flailing our arms against the status quo or indiscriminately disrupting its processes, and thereby claim that we are being faithful to Christ.

But it is just as obvious that we cannot silence the voice of protest, the "No!" that paves the way for the alternative that we represent. Jesus did not compromise the ideal; he did not permit the light to be polluted. For once we back off from the radical alternative and water it down, we lose our power to become children of God.

There are two ways we may respond to the presence of evil within us and around us (assuming we don't wholeheartedly embrace it): we may accept it with reluctance, or we may repent. To the extent that we daily and desperately repent, we are of the light. To the extent that we accept evil as necessary, and therefore conclude that we no longer are called to weep for it, confess it, and confront it with the ideals of Christ, to that extent we ratify the crucifixion.

Let me apply this theory to the political sphere in order to clarify my position. We have heard talk of a "Great Society," supposedly consisting of justice and righteousness, prosperity and equality. Those of us who have had some acquaintance with the people who would stand to benefit the most from such a state of affairs know that the "Great Society" is a myth.

Even if all the governmental programs that were originally intended to usher in this era were implemented, the "Great Society" would remain a myth. This is not to deny that some approximate good has been generated, but the "conditions" that were envisioned and the "methods" that were employed were not radical enough. Indeed, the "Great Society" program was so nonradical that a majority of people voted for it in 1964. I was one of them and I would vote that way again, but I would never be so presumptuous to claim that I was voting for a truly "Great Society." You can't make a silk purse out of a sow's ear, the saying goes. If we accept a world of darkness as a given, we cannot embrace anything that such a world produces as "great" or even "good."

That which God produces is alone in its goodness, so we can never abandon the apartness, the holiness, of the kingdom of God. (Holy: "set apart and dedicated to the service or worship of God.") We can never equate the kingdom of God with a particular political program, nor can we ever embrace a political figure as a social "messiah." Nothing that humanity initiates, no matter how relatively good it may be, is radical enough to command anything more than our passing allegiance. The problem with calling any society "great" or any era a "generation of peace" is that we leave no room in our vocabulary for the terminology of the kingdom. The difference between the peace that our politicians offer and the peace of Jesus Christ is so drastic that we Christians may have to revert to the use of the Hebrew term "shalom" until even that is confiscated and vulgarized by secular thought.

But the problem is more than just one of semantics. The fact is that we have begun, in our country, to equate approximate truth with Truth, and we have decided to sanctify the status quo in lieu of holding out for the "impossible" alternative of the kingdom of God. The word *radical* has become a dirty word in our society, but we must strive to salvage it or else come up with a synonym. We can't abandon the radical nature of our faith. While there is much that goes by the name *radical* that is not Christian, there is absolutely nothing that is Christian that is not also radical.

When we Christians maintain a business-as-usual type of life, we are really saying that either the kingdom of God has arrived, or it is an unreachable goal that we are not asked to implement in this life. In the former case we are revealing a profound ignorance of the "conditions" and "methods" of either this world or the kingdom. In the latter case we are sidestepping the New Testament call to discipleship.

Nothing that I have observed within the Christian community causes greater anguish than the fact that we have lost our appreciation of what God demands of us and of our world. We have baptized the American way of life. There is therefore no need for radical change. Nor is there opportunity even to weep for our culture. We get the picture that if Jesus came today he would find more reason to honor America than to call her to repentance and faith. Perhaps no one would say that our righteousness is perfect, but many would say that it is impressive, and certainly a far cry from the biblical concept that our righteousness is as "filthy rags" (Isa 64:6, KJV).

If you have not yet come to see that to be a Christian is to be a radical, then you will not derive much from the remainder of this writing. My purpose now is to discover the type of radicalism that is uniquely Christian.

2. The Kingdom as a Gift

ONE INCONSISTENCY MAY HAVE occurred to the reader thus far. I have talked about the need to be radical while admitting that the kingdom of God will never truly arrive until Christ returns. Isn't radicalism, then, a futile exercise?

But the reader assumes that I espouse radicalism because I want to accomplish something, namely, the kingdom of God. I labor under no such illusion. I do not read in the New Testament where I am called upon to "build" the kingdom. The kingdom is normally spoken of as a given, something that is already here, in the sense that Jesus has planted its seed within every believer, and something that will also be fully realized when God intervenes at the end of history.

The kingdom exists for us in two tenses, present and future, but in neither case does it exist because we have initiated it or accomplished it. We are called upon to enter the kingdom now and to receive it in the future. These acts on our part are not passive (we must enter the kingdom "violently," that is, with abrupt change being caused thereby, and we must receive the kingdom as "little children," that is, with enthusiasm and simplicity, as a gift from a father). But these acts are not creative in the sense that we may be said to create the kingdom by entering it or receiving it.

The kingdom does not depend upon us. Rather, we depend upon the kingdom. Our radicalism consists in being true to kingdom principles at all times and places, being transformed by the renewal of our minds, so that we carry out on earth the will of the Father that is already complete in heaven, regardless of present adversities or consequences.

The person who is a radical because he wants to accomplish something begins with a problem. He may have a very correct understanding of the problem. He concludes that in an effort to solve the problem (let us say, the problem of poverty) radical action is necessary. He strategizes an approach that will induce the rich to share their substance with the poor. His radicalism is effective in so far as he accomplishes his goal. In this case, he winds up being frustrated. He may consider other approaches, perhaps violent ones, which will supposedly advance his cause.

I do not want to falsely characterize this person as totally naive, but I do believe he is misguided, at least in his attempt to eradicate poverty. For him the future is uncertain, it is the good future that he wants to secure. His concept of the future and of what it must be motivates his present action. He is working under unbearable pressure that drains the joy and the spontaneity from his life. In a very real sense, he is not free. His concept of the future dictates his present action, because its realization depends upon his present action just as an effect depends upon its cause.

I believe Jesus was throwing a bit of cold water on this approach when he said to Judas, "For you always have the poor with you" (Matt 25:11, JB). He was not saying that we should not be concerned for the poor, but Judas was permitting his concern, assuming it was sincere, to dictate his reaction to the woman who was anointing Jesus' body with precious ointment. His results-oriented mentality forced him to say, "This ointment might have been sold for a large sum, and given to the poor" (Matt 26:9, JB). Jesus did not rebuke him for his compassion, but for his naiveté, for his anxiety, for his inability to see that this woman had done a beautiful thing. Judas had been victimized by his radical nature. It controlled him and effected within him a nitpicking uptightness about life. No wonder he later became totally disenchanted with Jesus' approach.

The Christian who follows the approach of Jesus is a radical not because of his analysis of the problem, but because of his understanding of the person of Christ and his kingdom. This is a vital difference. He is not motivated so much by a problem as by a promise. The promise is: "The kingdom is yours." If you believe that promise, the natural outflow of your life will be a disciplined radicalism. You will not be a radical because you are trying to create a future, but because you have accepted the certainty of a reality that in turn is creating your own life. The promise of a future mercy, for example, permits us to be merciful today. The future penetrates, conditions, and produces the present, rather than vice versa.

I submit that the outlook on life of a man or a woman who is absolutely convinced of the promises of God will make him or her a dangerous revolutionary for Jesus Christ. A spontaneous radical spirit will blossom within, to the extent that one will be free to lay down one's life for the sake of the kingdom.

If someone had laid up for me in trust an inheritance of a million dollars that was to be mine some day, I would be free today to give all my money away. And this is precisely what I should believe and what I should do. I am a radical to the extent that I truly believe. I do not have to do anything, really, other than believe. That is a dangerous statement to make, because so many will take shelter in their "belief" and excuse their whole lives of complacency. But our belief must be the basis for our lives in order to be valid. Jesus made a similarly dangerous statement once when he said, "This is working for God: You must believe in the one he has sent" (John 6:29, JB).

The problem with the Christian community today is not that it is apathetic and unconcerned. These are only symptoms of the problem. The basic problem is that we don't believe God.

A related meaning of the term *radical* is, according to Webster, "of or pertaining to the root, proceeding from the root." In mathematics, for instance, a radical is the root of a number. A radish is an edible root. A radical person is someone who is rooted in something that is itself radical. Show me where the roots of a tree penetrate, and I will tell you the quantity and quality of fruit that the tree produces. In a sense, I only need to know about the root; I am not interested in the fruit.

The question for us is the question Jesus asked in Luke 18:8 (JB), "But when the Son of Man comes, will he find any faith on earth?" Of all the questions that Jesus might ask, this is the only one that really needs asking. For if you have faith, then you will naturally become poor in spirit, mournful, meek, hungry and thirsty for righteousness, merciful, pure in heart, a peacemaker, persecuted (Matt 5:1–12).

The commandment of God to love one's neighbor as one's self is burdensome only to those who do not know that they themselves are loved by God. If we understood the compassion that Christ has for us, we would be free to be compassionate. And the good works that would spontaneously flow from our lives would bear witness to the radical alternative of the kingdom and its Lord.

Acts 1:6 (JB) records the question that perhaps was asked by Jesus' disciples many times: "Lord, has the time come? Are you going to restore the kingdom to Israel?" The Lord replied, "It is not for you to know times or dates that the Father has decided by his own authority, but you will receive power when the Holy Spirit comes on you, and then you will be my witnesses."

Every day Christians are tempted to accept some strategy for the arrival of the kingdom. The strategy may go something like this: "If we do such and such, then such and such will happen. But then so and so may do this and that." The options may be carried out forever. You see that we are reasoning from the present into a tentative future. Because tomorrow bears so many contradictory possibilities, which no one can foresee, we usually are stymied from ever acting according to the leading of the Spirit. We are not to be leaderless; we are to be led by the Spirit. But we are to forego any full-fledged attempt at strategizing our progress. We are not to be concerned about anything other than today's compassionate witness. We are to seek the kingdom of God today. We may be sure that tomorrow's evil awaits us, but the only way we can be overwhelmed by tomorrow is by permitting it to govern what we do today (Matt 6:33–34). The ultimate future is known to the Christian. The future belongs eventually to God. Therefore, the only unknown about which we are to be concerned is today's faithfulness.

Jesus brings this out in the story of the Good Samaritan (Luke 10:29–37). The priest and the Levite who hastened by were perhaps well motivated in their desire to avoid involvement. They undoubtedly had many important and worthwhile things to do. But the immediate issue is really the only issue for the Christian that demands obedience. If we are concerned about the consequences of faith to the extent that they determine present action or inaction, then we are living not by faith, but by a calculating reason that shuts off the possibility for faith. As Clarence Jordan said, "Faith is living in scorn of consequences."

Unfortunately, many Christian activists share with their socially conservative brothers an incorrect methodology. They are both strategists. I believe God is concerned more about our immediate faithfulness than our long-range accomplishments or non-accomplishments. The servant who received the one talent and buried it in the ground was victimized by his view of what would happen if . . . (Matt 25:14–30). He was a conservative. That is, he wanted to conserve his talent no matter what. The disciples, on the other hand, had such a high view of the importance of their kingdom movement that they could not permit their revolutionary leader to be waylaid by a group of little children (Luke 18:15–17). They were radicals whose compelling concept of the need for change did not allow them to seize the present opportunity to implement the kingdom.

Strategies for converting the world and accomplishing social justice are at best temporary tools for the Christian. They may give some limited insight concerning the wisdom of a present course. But I would offer as an almost infallible rule that if you are guided for any length of time by any continuous strategy for either your own life or your organization, then chances are you are following some pagan wisdom. God never seems to give us broad outlines in advance, and we do well not to devise them for ourselves. The bigger barns that we build may not be filled with grain (Luke 12:16–21). They may contain grand redemptive schemes to be unleashed with precision timing for maximum effect. But the only question we really need ask is, "What does today's faithfulness require of me?"

There is great freedom and simplicity in living for today's kingdom possibilities. Unlike tomorrow, the ethical imperatives of today should not be a mystery to us. For example:

"Offer the wicked man no resistance. On the contrary, if anyone hits you on the right cheek, offer him the other as well; if a man takes you to law and would have your tunic, let him have your cloak as well. And if anyone orders you to go one mile, go two miles with him. Give to anyone who asks, and if anyone wants to borrow, do not turn away" (Matthew 5:39–42, JB).

"And as you go, proclaim that the kingdom of heaven is close at hand. Cure the sick, raise the dead, cleanse the lepers, cast out devils. You received without charge, give without charge" (Matt 10:7–8, JB)

"What will all this accomplish?" you ask. That is left to God. We do these things and others because we are rooted in the rich soil of the kingdom. What happens tomorrow may not reveal our wisdom, and any good that we accomplish will probably be swallowed up by 'existing . . . conditions." But we believe more deeply in the final vindication of the kingdom ethic than in the apparent circumstances of history.

I am writing these things because I believe there is a great deal of Christian radicalism that isn't radical enough. I remember the television game show that was entitled *Truth or Consequences*. I'm sure this wasn't the point of the show, but it is my point: when we are most concerned with truth, we will have little concern for consequences, and vice versa. I am convinced that the early Christians turned the world upside down partly because they didn't devote too much effort to figuring out how to do it. Christian radicals, myself included, spend time taking the pulse to see how strong the movement is. Our real strength lies in our ability to respond with a spontaneous faithfulness to daily circumstances and let the movement take care of itself.

A group of students on the Fuller Theological Seminary campus put up an anti-Vietnam War display. They had received proper clearance to do so. A professor who was of the opposite persuasion about the war saw the signs and immediately took them down.

Many of us were incensed at this un-American authoritarianism that denied our freedom of speech. There was some thought of marching right up to that professor's office, venting our rage, and perhaps forcefully replacing the display. The anger was justified, and certainly it was right to explain to the professor our disagreement with his action.

It was indeed a radical thought to advocate love of our enemies. The purpose of the display was to communicate the non-Christian way in which our country was relating to the situation in Vietnam. But while we were making a radical stance for brotherly love toward the people of Indochina, we came close to exhibiting a very non-radical contempt for a man who had at least at this point become our enemy. In other words, we were radical in principle, while in our personal actions and thoughts we came close to adopting the "traditional views, habits, conditions . . . and methods" of spiteful revenge.

That is what happens to so many of us would-be radicals. We pass by the personal opportunities for turning the other cheek and for loving our enemies, because we are concerned to take a public stance. We forget the darkness that is within us, where radical confrontation must begin. By all means let us continue our open advocacy for social righteousness. But let us not overlook the daily opportunities for personal faithfulness to the kingdom of God and to our brothers and sisters. More kingdom opportunities will come our way by accident than by design.

A brief passage from Hebrews gives insight into the truly radical attitude and action of at least some of the early church:

> Remember all the sufferings that you had to meet after you received the light, in earlier days; sometimes by being yourselves publicly exposed to insults and violence, and sometimes as associates of others who were treated in the same way. For you not only shared in the sufferings of those who were in prison, but you happily accepted being stripped of your belongings, knowing that you owned something that was better and lasting" (Heb 10:32–35, JB).

The persecution that came to them must have destroyed whatever strategy they may have had for the orderly communication of the gospel and for the application of their resources to social betterment. But these disruptive adversities only served to dramatize the difference between the nonbeliever and the believer, or, more pointedly, between the Christian who is oriented toward potential results and the Christian who is grounded in the promised kingdom.

If I had the chance to rewrite the Ten Commandments, I would be tempted to slip in the words, "Thou shalt not be anxious. Thou shalt not be a strategist. Thou shalt not be primarily concerned with consequences." But really these words are already implied in the introduction of the commandments: "I am Yahweh your God who brought you out of the land of Egypt, out of the house of slavery" (Exod 20:2, JB). This is the one we trust, whose kingdom we represent.

When we lay down our arms before our enemies, we are saying, "I trust God." When we give away tomorrow's security for the sake of meeting someone else's need today, we are saying, "God is my security." When we rejoice in the impoverishment and imprisonment that our world wishes upon us, we are saying, "Our abundance and our freedom are in Christ and his kingdom." This is the simple, unshakable trust that constitutes our radical witness to the world.

The kingdom of God in relation to this world is infinitely radical. There must be a constant desperate seeking of the kingdom for our lives and implementing of its teachings in our relationships. The Sermon on the Mount gives an excellent sampling of divine imperatives for this life. It is not a picture of the future kingdom, but of the present kingdom in tension with the world of darkness. (As evidence of this, we need only note that the Beatitudes make mention of elements that will not be relevant to the final kingdom, such as mourning (Matt 5:5) and persecution (5:10).) Every nonradical Christian ethic may be dismissed as phony. Everyone who has made his peace with this world is an enemy of God.

But our practice of these truths is incomplete if we are motivated by the noble ends that we hope to achieve. The world will probably dash our hopes and leave us with our frustration. The good and faithful servant is the one who loves because he is of the Father, who gives because he is possessed by the mind of Christ, who becomes oppressed because God in Christ has become one with the oppressed. The fulfillment and joy of the disciple come from the measure of his faithfulness, regardless of his accomplishment. Our gentleness, our mercy, are best understood not as means to ends, but as simple reflections of the kingdom mentality.

This spirit is the unique essence of the radicalism of Jesus. He healed the ten lepers because it was his nature to be compassionate. Only one of them returned to give thanks (Luke 17:11-19), but he did not heal them as a strategy to win their allegiance. His joy was full because he had done the will of the Father, and that was sufficient for him.

May we also discover the secret of this naive non-strategy. Our accountability is to God, not to tomorrow, not to history. The world touches us deeply with its need, but it has no judgment to impose upon us, no potential results for us to achieve, no model to measure our efficiency.

And therein lies our freedom. If we understand that freedom, we will show the world what it means to be radical.

II

THE RADICAL CHURCH

3. SERVANTHOOD

THE FOLLOWING IS THE summation of much thought and prayer regarding our mission and calling as Christians. Intertwined in my thoughts will be considerations of our individual roles and our corporate role. I am writing to you as brothers and sisters in Christ who are struggling as I am to understand and implement the will of God. I am aware that we are all at different levels of growth. I don't want to impose my level of understanding on you, but I do want you to seriously and openly consider my convictions just as I reconsider them. I sense that the Lord is leading us together into a renewing of our lives. We need each other in order to be faithful to him.

At one point I would have broken down my thoughts into two main areas: the proclamation of the gospel and the implementation of the gospel. I now believe that breakdown to be impossible in light of the New Testament. Jesus spoke of his mission in this way in the fourth chapter of Luke: "The spirit of the Lord has been given to me for he has anointed me. He has sent me to bring the good news to the poor, to proclaim liberty to captives and to the blind new sight, to set the downtrodden free, to proclaim the Lord's year of favour" (4:18–19, JB).

It is clear that Jesus fulfilled the "Lord's year of favour" as he proclaimed it. In fact, throughout the Scripture the Word of God is pictured as a force that accomplishes what it proclaims in one continuous action: "He said, 'Let there be light,' and there was light." "He uttered His voice, and the earth melted." "He said, 'Peace, be still,'" and the waves subsided. He did not proclaim good news without bringing it, or sight without giving it. I believe, despite what we see happening in our world, that we are still in the "Lord's year of favour." This is the year, now extended into over 2000 years, when the power of God is available through the body of Christ to minister to the world. We follow in the same way as Jesus Christ, anointed by the same Holy Spirit to the same ministry.

The final phrase of the Isaiah passage that Jesus quoted at the beginning of his mission is "to proclaim a year of favour from Yahweh, a day of vengeance for our God" (61:2, JB). He deliberately omitted the last portion because the "day of vengeance" has not yet come. It is well to remind ourselves, however, that we work, as he did, in the shadow of that coming day when the "Lord's year of favour" will end for those who have not become his followers. The day of vengeance will test the quality of each of our lives, to see whether, as Paul says, we have built with gold, silver, and jewels or with wood, grass, and straw.

Someone said to me this week that when he met Jesus Christ for the first time, he came to the realization that 90 percent of his life up until then had been wasted. I am concerned that when I meet Jesus Christ for the final time, notwithstanding my sure salvation, I may discover that 90 percent of my Christian life has been similarly wasted, with abortive proclamation.

This writing, and the life that it hopefully represents, reflects my continuing attempt to work out that proclamation, that is, to implement my own salvation, with fear and trembling. The determination to hear him someday say to me, "Well done, thou good and faithful servant," (Matt 25:21, KJV) overrides the fears and misgivings that all of us have regarding the potential earthly consequences of discipleship.

I believe that God is calling each of us to a ministry of teaching, in one form or another. We must begin to articulate thoroughly and comprehensively the Word of God to our generation. We cannot get by with piecemeal interpretation of isolated events in the life of Christ. Although such glimpses might be appropriate for talks and sermons that whet the appetite, they cannot become our full bill of fare. The people of the Old Testament perished for lack of knowledge, even though they were familiar with the stories of Yahweh, from Adam to David. Our society is perishing because it is honestly ignorant of Yahweh and of the Lord Jesus, except in a superficial sense.

Of course, if we truly understood Jesus, we would understand Yahweh, as might our fellow Christians. But we seldom speak to them of the Jesus who cursed the fig tree and who cleansed the temple, who condemned the hypocrites of his day and disassociated himself from the well-wishers and the sympathizers who wanted to remain on the periphery of his movement, with one foot in the old order. And so Jesus becomes to us as an easy dispenser of grace in the form of healing miracles, and we forget that he later cursed the very towns that had seen the most of his power:

> Alas for you, Chorazin! Alas for you, Bethsaida! For if the miracles done in you had been done in Tyre and Sidon, they would have repented long ago in sackcloth and ashes. And still, I tell you that it will not go as hard on judgment day with Tyre and Sidon as with you. And as for you, Capernaum, did you want to be exalted as high as heaven? You shall be thrown down to hell. For if the miracles done in you had been done in Sodom, it would have been standing yet. And still, I tell you that it will not go as hard with the land of Sodom on judgment day as with you (Matt 11:20–24, JB).

And as for you, Christian church! And as for you, Bill Lane Doulos! Have you seen anything of God's grace in your life? Have you tasted his goodness? Has his grace been interpreted by you as a call to obedience or as a substitute for obedience? Has his grace only relieved your fears, or has it also taught your heart to fear? As the writer to the Hebrews says: "We have been given possession of an unshakable kingdom. Let us therefore hold on to the grace we have been given and use it to worship God in the way that he finds acceptable, in reverence and fear. For our God is a consuming fire" (12:28–29, JB).

This is the whole knowledge of God, that he is a gracious God of consuming fire. We must learn and convey that knowledge to our generation. We are largely ignorant of the demand for acceptable worship that is inherent in God's grace. Jesus reserved his harshest words for those whose assurance of God's grace easily relieved their fears and led them to casually overlook the weightier matters of the law: justice, kindness, and humility. The worship that God demands of us does not consist of right liturgy, or right words, but of right actions.

I believe his call to us centers on three areas of action: servanthood, community, and celebration. I want to lead our thoughts in these three areas.

Even though Jesus is the personification of servanthood, the church that he founded is almost completely unconscious of what servanthood means. Let me make a somewhat artificial distinction between "helping" someone and being someone's servant. The two concepts are actually radically different. Someone who "helps" does so from a position of superiority. We "help" the poor by giving a percentage of our income. We "help" the lonely by visiting them. We "help" the spiritually lost by introducing them to Jesus Christ.

In the Old Testament God "helped" his people. He gave them the law and the prophets; he sent them manna from heaven; he gave them a land flowing with milk and honey. Most of the time we live, and we challenge our brothers to live, under the Old Testament concept of giving. For in all of these Old Testament circumstances, God retained his superiority; he retained his control of the situation; he retained his security.

The scandal of the New Testament is the cross, that is, the servanthood of God—God no longer in the heavens, God given over to the will of men, God vulnerable to the world. This is not just a greater amount of help; this is not just giving 100 percent of one's possessions rather than 10 percent. This is a qualitative difference. This is beyond "giving" and "helping."

This is becoming one with the oppressed, the lonely, the poor, the naked. It is significant that Jesus uses the cross as the supreme symbol of New Testament discipleship and that Paul conjures up the image of the cross when he asks us to present ourselves as a living sacrifice, for this is the only worship that is reasonable and acceptable to God.

There are some who will present themselves at the judgment as church leaders and counselors. God does not know you. You proclaimed but did not implement. Some will present themselves as helpers of mankind. You cast out demons. God does not know you. You helped, but you retained your life in the process. Some will come as little children, that is, with no credentials, only a pedigree: born of the Spirit. You will inherit the kingdom prepared for you. As we bear one another's burdens—as we become burdened—we fulfil the law, the example, and the command of Christ (Gal 6:2).

I am only beginning to experience the changes that the cross brings to my life. I suspect that it should bring many changes to your life and to the church as well. The concept of servanthood has begun to simplify my life. Much of what used to be meaningful to me has lost its determining role in my existence. I am no longer caught up with the necessity to read books or to attend meetings or to write letters or to make speeches. I am no longer concerned with the strategy of winning the world for Christ. I no longer share the organizational consciousness of the Christian movement.

Of course I am overstating my progress (and one might be accurate in saying that I am inventing my progress), but I am citing the *process* of freedom that has begun to influence my daily decisions. The structure of my life, the structure of discipleship itself, is becoming meaningless to me. If this disqualifies me from my present work, that is no concern of mine. I do know that I am becoming qualified for the cross because my energies are freed up to serve people, rather than organizations, or standards, or preconceived ideas. I am led by the Spirit day by day as to how I can best love both friends and enemies, those who hold my convictions and those who oppose them. But I am not a slave to ultimate concepts or doctrines or positions.

It is true that I will pay my taxes this year (1971) under protest, because in my own feeble way I am trying to love the people of Vietnam. I have begun living in the inner city, because I find more concrete opportunity to love my neighbor there. I have joined John Gardner's Common Cause organization, because I have found it to be a chance to register an intelligent love for the people of my country. I have divested myself of my savings, because many people have needed my money more than I do. I have begun the process of servanthood, not because I have some compelling theology of discipleship, but because I love Jesus Christ and I want to share his life. I know that I am being led inevitably to the time and place where I will stand completely empty before God, penniless and dispossessed, that I might complete in my body the sufferings of Christ.

We may take the church to the country clubs and the suburbs, and we may love people there just as Jesus loved Mary and Martha and Lazarus in suburban Bethany. But we must recognize that we are going into a foreign world when we do so. If we want people to see the love of Christ in continuous demonstration, we must take them into our own homes and onto our turf, where people are concerned with serving one another rather than impressing one another, where human needs are met in a modest way, and where the races and the classes mix without distinction.

4. COMMUNITY

As we begin to serve one another and as we begin to serve the world, I believe we will begin naturally to obey a second aspect of our calling: a calling into community.

If we truly follow in the way of the cross, the world will begin to distinguish us as Christians. We will become a threat once more to the standards of a pagan culture and to the concept of "giving" of a pagan church. We will be more and more cut off from union with our world although we are still called to penetrate it with the love of Jesus Christ. Our separation will be effected by silent ostracism and perhaps by open persecution. We will not be able to hold jobs that demand subjection to what Charles Reich has called the "corporate state" and what Theodore Roszak has called "objective consciousness." Perhaps society will find us unsuitable for any but the most menial occupations. We will perhaps literally become her servants—washing her dishes and carrying her garbage. We will be truly fulfilling our role as the salt of the earth—the light of the world that shines in the darkness, and that the darkness cannot put out.

Of course, the structure of the church will change. The poor, the blind, and the lame will form our boards, our support, and our staff. Perhaps our work in the suburbs will pass away for want of an audience. People's ears will grow dull to the truth. Perhaps our church buildings will be sold and the money given to the poor. But in the midst of our evolution as the people of God, a remnant of our society will be saved. And the people whose needs are visible and offensive to the rest of society will flock to us as they came to the Christ 2,000 years ago. In the context of this redemptive and obedient community, I believe God will pour out his spirit as never before to empower us for the mission that is now beginning to open up to us.

But community is not something the world will force upon us; it is something that we seek for ourselves. It is part of the calling of Christ. To think of community in terms of living and eating together is not my concern here, although that may well be for some of us an appropriate outward manifestation of a spiritual reality. The point is that I have come to realize how much we need each other and how much we belong to each other. I have come to know that I have no claim on myself higher than the claim that many of you have on me and on my life. And I have come to experience a divine fulfillment in this growing relationship.

We need to confess to one another, to pray with one another, to be security and collateral for each other in time of need, to share our joys and our sorrows, and to discipline and encourage as each deals with personal sin and as all of us together struggle against the sin of our culture.

5. CELEBRATION!

As SERVANTHOOD LEADS US into community, community leads us into celebration.

Few of us realize the part that celebration plays in the life of discipleship. We tend to think that celebration is something that is out of keeping with the life of the suffering servant. But celebration is at the foundation of our lives together and serves to distinguish us even further from the world. The world celebrates to ease its pain and its awareness of the absurdity of life. But the community of Christ celebrates to remind itself of the true reality of life—the kingdom of God. We do not seek to escape the difficulty of servanthood or the reality of the world's misery. But in the midst of that reality, we celebrate in obedience to one of the first commandments God gave to his people.

The people of the Old Testament were to observe six days of labor, but on the seventh day they were to rest from their labor and enter into the promises of God, even though those promises had not been fully realized. The kingdom, with its joy and celebration, was to penetrate their difficult and frustrating lives, giving them a taste of a future that would be without sorrow, a reality that was more ultimate, more real, than their present circumstances. That is why the creation account describes the seventh day as a day without morning or evening, without beginning or end—an eternal day that represents the fulfillment of God's plan.

Every seventh year was a Sabbath year, and at the end of seven sets of seven years, that is, every fiftieth year, there was a year of

Jubilee. Prisoners were freed, debts were cancelled, and land was returned to its original owner. The reform program of every Leftist group in the world today is thus foreshadowed in the Old Testament. But the Left labels their revolution as "Power to the People." That is why they will never succeed in "proclaiming liberty to the captives" or "healing to the brokenhearted." Jesus initiates and fulfills this revolution because he correctly gives to God the kingdom, and the power, and the glory.

The Christian community has no right to celebrate the Sabbath unless it participates in its six days of labor. Jesus defined the content of those six days as his servanthood and his cross. We are to drink the same cup of suffering. But in the midst of Jesus' ministry, in the midst of pouring out his life, he would call his little group together, and they would celebrate.

Their celebrations were so extravagant that the straight world would think that this was a band of gluttons and winebibbers. The actions of Jesus would be labeled inappropriate for a prophet who was supposedly concerned with the poor and the hungry. In the midst of the pressures and sorrows, Jesus remembered the Sabbath principle. The religious leaders of Jesus' time completely misinterpreted the Sabbath as a day of mourning and restraint. But for six days we are to mourn; for six days we are to restrain and discipline ourselves; we are to subject ourselves to every legitimate human need. Then we come to the day that "was made for man," the day that recognizes, in advance of the historical moment, that Jesus Christ is Lord.

Just as Jesus did with his community, we are to gather ourselves together at regular intervals, perhaps in families or in groups of two or three at the end of every day, perhaps around the Lord's table once a week, perhaps away from the city or the classroom sometime each month. And we are to bind up one another's wounds, confess our sins, renew our spirits, give thanks and praise to God, and, in remembrance of the Sabbath and of Jesus Christ, we are to celebrate.

And this is not a luxury for us. This is a necessity. Unless our lives are in the approximate ratio of six parts servitude to one part celebration, we are being disobedient. By celebrating the Lord's death until he comes, we are reminding ourselves and proclaiming to the world that the cross is our glory, that death is the passageway to life, and that the sufferings of this present day are not worth comparing to the glory that will be revealed to us.

Each of us must flesh out in his or her own life the implications of servanthood, of community, and of celebration. I am not trying to impose upon you a theory of discipleship. I have only tried to paint a broad picture of where we might find ourselves someday if we are faithful. The important thing is not to be faithful to a concept of the future. That would be a burden too great for any of us. The important thing is to be obedient to the immediate step of faith that today is impinging upon your life.

Although you may be confused or dismayed by the thoughts that I have presented, I believe that there is one burden that God is clearly asking you to bear, and that you have the power to pick up. Don't be faithful to my description of servanthood, but ask God to reveal to you one human need that you have the resources to meet. Then, as you begin to empty yourself of your resources, as you lose your life, you will begin to fall into community and cry out for celebration.

None of us has arrived. But we press on . . . to know him, to know the power of his resurrection, to know the fellowship of his suffering. It is one thing to "know him." But that knowledge is only the tip of the iceberg. Most of the people who claim to be Christians never proceed any further than that initial knowledge. The richest treasure remains beneath the surface, where we are welded together as a community that celebrates his power as we share his suffering.

When we go beyond the superficial, we begin to realize that his grace is amazing in two ways: amazing because of what it gives and amazing because of what it demands.

Jesus began his ministry by "proclaiming" good news to the poor, healing to the brokenhearted, liberty to the captives, freedom to the downtrodden—in short, by proclaiming the year of the Lord's favor. Three years later he ended his ministry. He was poor, he was brokenhearted, he was a captive, he was downtrodden. He had experienced the day of vengeance of our God.

If that was a defeat, then let us avoid this man Jesus Christ at all costs; if it was a victory, then let us begin to pay the same price, so that we can have the same glory in our lives. And let us follow as a joyous community, thanking God for his Son, and for each other.

6. New Directions for the Church

I speak of the evangelical Christian community as my spiritual home. That is where my roots are and most of my current relationships (1972). That is also where I feel most at home doctrinally. However, in the important arena of Christian action, I feel as a stranger to my own heritage.

I believe that right action proceeds from right doctrine. This concept compels us to have an initial concern with right doctrine, which is the source for ethics. But I have little sympathy for a person whose right doctrine does not produce right action. I do not believe right doctrine is a virtue in its own right. Most of Paul's letters in the New Testament begin with doctrinal clarification and end with ethical implementation. This is as it should be in our own lives. "To believe" in the New Testament refers to a vital life-force belief, not an intellectual elitism. Right doctrine for its own sake has always been an abomination to God. The Old Testament prophets did not primarily emphasize doctrinal reformation. They attacked the ethical outworking of doctrine to show that the beliefs themselves were hollow. Faith without works has always been dead. What does it profit a man if he has faith to move mountains? What regard is there for those who call, "Lord, Lord . . . ."? Better that the doors to the temple be shut than that the people of God profane his house with superficial sacrifice and hollow worship. Satan himself believes, and trembles.

My basic challenge to the Christian community is the challenge to live according to its beliefs. I do not desire to change its beliefs, but to illumine them and activate them. I am convinced that if the church were to take the lordship of Christ seriously, we would find a new power to our proclamation. But I frankly have mixed emotions about our present proclamation to the world. The words are right; the context is wrong. And so the words are pacifiers.

When Jesus says from the cross, "Father, forgive them," his words change mankind. He has won the right to be heard. Take the same message, engrave it in gold, preach it from prestige positions around the world, and the revolution dies as the ears of millions of listeners turn deaf.

I have trouble handling the anger within me as I consider the monstrosity of an affluent church. Even as I write this I have to pause between sentences. I have to choose the third or fourth phrase that comes to mind because the first ones are too abusive and arrogant. If the result of whatever I say is constructive I will be grateful for the measureless grace of God.

Jesus came "to bring the good news to the poor, to proclaim liberty to captives and to the blind new sight, to set the downtrodden free, to proclaim the Lord's year of favour" (Luke 4:18–19, JB). My first major ethical difference with the Christian community is that it has abandoned the ones Jesus came to help. It has fled to the suburbs and then tacked on to its mission budget a few inner-city projects to relieve its guilt.

Of course there are oppressed people everywhere. But by every criterion the lower class is the greatest victim of oppression in our culture today. When Jesus was asked why he ate with tax collectors and sinners he replied, "It is not the healthy who need the doctor, but the sick" (Matt 9:12, JB). Of course no one is "well" in an ultimate sense. But there are those who by the world's standards are "well" and there are those who are "sick." The "sick" may be well-off financially, as the tax collectors were, but they have some stigma attached to their lives. If not poverty, it may be mental or physical handicap, criminal tendencies, alcoholism, drug addiction, acute loneliness, sickness. These people for the most part are lower class and urban.

Why is the nature of the church and its related nondenominational ministries largely middle class and suburban? I do not see a biblical mandate for exclusiveness in favor of either the rich or the poor. Jesus had relations with all. But where were his priorities? The people who populate our ministries and sit in our pews are in great contrast to the people of early Christendom. "Those whom the world thinks common and contemptible are the ones that God has chosen" (1 Cor 1:28, JB). But we, being wiser than God and more shrewd in our strategy of changing the world, have chosen the rich to be on our boards, the respectable to lead our grassroots work. And our mission field? Also the respectable, the influential, the college-bound, the business person.

When God comes to raise up the valleys and level the mountains, when many who are now first become last and the last first, how much prestige and acceptance will our work have in the eyes of God? I believe we must become much more concerned than we are with the "lower class" of society.

A second disagreement I have with our posture in the world is that we are aligned with the status quo of government, business, and educational institutions. Evangelicals, including myself, have always felt that the way to deal with corporate sin is by dealing with individual sin. First change the human heart, then the culture will be changed. But because the evangelical community has failed to recognize the implications of corporate institutional sin, its doctrine of individual salvation has become emasculated.

There is a concept in Scripture of the growth of wickedness. In the pages of Genesis we see that evil spread both before and after the days of Noah, despite the salvation which was visited upon Noah's family. Evil is clearly more than the sum total of human sin. There are principalities and powers that are in control, says Paul. Salvation is basic, but there are ramifications to salvation that encompass the entire groaning universe. There are new men and women now, but salvation is not complete for anyone until there are also a new heavens and a new earth.

To begin with individual salvation is wise and biblical. It is unwise and unbiblical to take a newborn babe in Christ and to feed him to the ravenous world and think that somehow we are leavening the loaf. If a member of the Mafia came to our church and accepted Christ as Lord and Savior, we could not expect him to survive as a Christian in the world of the Mafia. We could not very well say to him, "Go back to the Mafia, and as you rob, kill, threaten, and exploit your brothers and sisters, try to have a Christian influence on the people with whom you work."

We would have to create an alternative culture for him, and that in itself would be a powerful witness to his business partners. What are the neutral occupations and the neutral institutions in our society? Can we send the bankers back to the bank, the soldiers back to the front, the teachers and the students back to the classrooms, the doctors back, the judges, the lawyers, the legislators, the salesmen, the advertisers, the preachers? Has not wickedness converted even the time-honored professions into a jungle of compromise, violence, exploitation, and the survival of the fittest? This is perhaps an extreme statement of the case, but this is clearly an accurate statement of the trend in our society and thus sufficient mandate for us to generate alternative structures—institutions that are humane, systems where Christians are free to be compassionate servants.

When the church in the first century was declared illegal, when it dispersed and went underground, it was the light of the world. When Constantine declared Christianity to be the religion of the state in the early fourth century, when the state embraced it and made it a partner in the status quo, the very light became darkness. Separation of church and state means much more today than no prayer in public schools. The ecclesia, the "called-out ones," must resist the old and build the new. The old way of life that is left behind is dirty thoughts and foul language. It is also fishing nets, zealotism, and tax collecting. The church must once again become a resistance movement.

The church has lost credibility with the world and, more importantly, with God, because of its relative power and affluence. This situation points out my third and most basic point of disagreement. The church has adopted the role of master in its abortive attempt to follow in the footsteps of a Messiah who resisted that role (cf. Matt 1:8–10). It has stooped to help the unfortunate from a position of financial security that parallels the glory of God the Son before he became a man. In his pre-humiliation state, Christ had the privileges of God and deservedly so (cf. Phil 2:6). It was not guilt but compassion that led him to final vulnerability, emptiness, and poverty.

The church today has a certain glory in society, prestige, and privileges encompassing far more than the monetary. All of these are to be offered up in the manner of Jesus Christ, out of compassion and without reservation. Does anyone doubt that the world for whom Christ died needs the infilling of the material and the spiritual that the modern-day crucifixion of the church would generate? If the church were biblical in action as well as doctrine, it would make the implementation of the cross an ethical priority. There is a difference between understanding the work of reconciliation and doing that work. The Third World yearns for the church to be the body of Christ broken and the blood poured out. The heart of the problem is a lack of faith—a lack of faith that humiliation gives way to exaltation. But the greatest symptom of the problem is that the church is well-fed among the hungry, well-housed among the refugees, and well-clothed among the naked.

What possible explanation can there be for a church that claims it has taken up its cross yet remains preserved and unscathed? I believe the explanation lies in an analysis of the continuous and stubborn reaction of the disciples when Jesus attempted to explain his passion to them. They simply could not understand how the crucifixion of the Messiah could be the wisdom of God. How can the death of Christ serve the kingdom? Does it not defeat the kingdom? Do we not need a strong church, endowed with human wisdom and resources that can defend itself against the never-ending onslaught of the needy? Is it possible for us to respond to humanity's every demand that the church give up its position of privilege and wealth?

The passion of Christ comes to each one of us. As the guards approach us in the garden, let no one of us draw the sword in

31

self-defense. As the pagan courts convict us, let no one of us speak in protestation. As the crowds crucify us, let us know what we are about even if they do not. We do not have a Messiah complex. We simply seek to share the cup of servanthood that he drank. What we accomplish as a church is only of secondary concern, but we can trust that women and men will be reconciled to God through the sacrifice of Christ as it becomes historically continuous with our lives. Our primary concern is to be true to our nature as daughters and sons of God, to flesh out in our own bodies the sufferings of Christ (Col 1:24).

Therein we become the people of God and the church is renewed.

I long for the church to take up its cross. Why has the doctrine of loving neighbor as oneself become so impotent in the bosom of the church? When will we come to an end of the defensiveness and the excuses of a church that preaches repentance to the pagan world while practicing self-righteousness? We are so creative when it comes to being a power broker in society and so zealous in the pursuit of self-preservation. How is it that our creativity and our zeal dissipate when it comes to dying? How is it that an institution that once was persecuted by the state has now been embraced and adopted by the powers that be? Have twenty centuries enlightened and mellowed the world so much that it no longer tries to put out the light? Or has the light itself been overcome by darkness? The damning questions can be put a thousand ways. They all point to the same disease.

The sick have been quarantined by a church that wants to avoid jeopardizing its own "health." The status quo has been embraced by those who are concerned that the "gospel" be preached in a benign atmosphere. The strategy of reconciliation through powerlessness has been sacrificed on the altar of "respectability." But the strategy has backfired and produced opposite results.

Remember the story of Jesus rebuking his disciples when they tried to protect him from the little children, the bothersome, the sick? Remember when the apostles said, "We must obey God rather than men"? Remember when Jesus said, "Follow me," and "He who does not renounce all that he has cannot be my disciple"? Buried underneath the rubble of modern-day Christian ethics, I believe there is that same capacity for commitment and compassion.

May the God who was gracious enough to redeem us be patient enough to remind us.

III

THE CHRISTIAN AND MATERIALISM

7. The Issue Before Us

THE TOPIC OF THE Christian and materialism has become more relevant today than ever before. The wealth of some countries has become staggering at the same time that the deprivation of other nations grows. Population increase has compounded the concern. Even within relatively wealthy countries there is a wide divergence between the rich and the poor. One does not have to be a social scientist to know that the problem exists or a theologian to know that it has relevance to contemporary Christian ethics.

A report from Seoul, Korea, is that the city's ten-year housing plan (1972) envisions the construction of sufficient dwellings that every citizen has enough space to sleep without having to cross his arms or legs to allow floor space for others.

A friend writes from Afghanistan:

> Our trip through the provinces was really disturbing for me. There's been a drought here and people are starving. When we got to a town named Herat, it was filled with beggars. We were told not to give because we would be mobbed and we didn't have enough to help anyway. I

> didn't give the first day, but I finally let down the second.
> I was carrying a bag of oranges, and I stopped to give one
> to a crippled boy by the road. Well, in a second I was sur-
> rounded by hundreds of beggars. I just dropped the bag
> and took off. I was lucky to get away. The crowd fought
> each other for the food.

Compassionate action begins when we relate to these people—the shack dwellers of our own country, the refugees of Asia, the Third World—as human beings. They are not "gooks," "niggers," "poor white trash," or statistics. Nor are they ideological enemies. They are families, loved ones, neighbors. If we would permit the Bible to teach us that—if we would enable our intuitive grasp of the brotherhood and sisterhood of men and women created in the image of God to vindicate the Bible's teaching—then the church's posture regarding materialism would be quickly rectified. But the church's heart is made of the same material as its sacred sanctuary. The church has accepted its sin of wealth in the midst of poverty for so long that it is doubtful that a clear vision of suffering mankind would do anything but confirm its wickedness.

It is significant that the Third World largely represents countries with colonial pasts. Is there any relationship between the poverty of the Third World and the wealth of the colonial powers? I think so. Is there a relationship between our wealth as a nation, the United States of America, and the manner in which we have exploited the African Americans and the Native Americans? Obviously!

On a trip across the country this past summer (1971), 1 passed through a small Mississippi town. The first half of the town was the black section. The roads were mostly dirt, the people were ill-clad, the river was filled with debris, and the houses were falling down. Then it was as if we passed through a looking glass. The river became lovely as it meandered past grassy banks. Modern and sometimes palatial homes were built on country-sized lots. The streets were well-paved. My guess would be that the mainline denominations exist only on the white side of town and that there are no blacks among their membership. My guess would be that their elders and their deacons live along the grassy banks. My guess would be that white, "Bible-believing" Christians are the rulers of this town and the primary beneficiaries of its southern comfort.

On paper, the biblical ethic is the most compassionate and humane ethic in the world. In actuality, Christian practice has become cruel and heartless. For this small Mississippi town is a microcosm of a world in which the white Christian community, of which I am a member, is largely master, and the nonwhite and non-believing majority of people is largely slave.

I have cited instances above that could be multiplied end-lessly to show conditions that should shame each one of us. My primary purpose, however, is not to shame us into action, but to build biblical conviction regarding the materialism of most of our lives. Each one of us must look critically and continuously at his or her lifestyle and ask if it reflects the mind of Christ. But the mind of Christ is not a mystery beyond our grasp. It is not an emotional, impulsive reaction that leads us to drop our bag of oranges and run as the ultimate in responsible Christian action. It is my purpose to examine the mind of Christ as it is revealed to us in God's Word.

Humankind's condition leaves us with our shame and our guilt and with the possibility of some brief and futile flurry of hu-manity. But the mind of Christ instills within us the possibility of being a creative channel of blessing to a needy world at the same time that we ourselves drink the blessed cup of Christ's suffering, experience personal fulfillment and redemption, and touch the heart of God.

The heart of God is historically continuous with the mind of Christ, which in turn is hopefully continuous with our own lives. There can be no contradiction between the purposes of Yahweh in the Old Testament and the earthly life of Jesus in the New. If we have the outline of God's plan in the Old, we have the fulfillment of God's plan in the incarnation, when God became flesh and lived among us. As we look at the Old Testament, we might utilize the words of Paul, "Now we see in a mirror dimly, but then [in the New] face to face" (1 Cor 13:12, RSV). The Old gives us a true glimpse of God in both his holiness and his love; the cross gives us the clear eternal presence of both.

8. THE WITNESS OF THE
OLD TESTAMENT LAW

LET US FIRST LOOK at the Old Testament for the emerging of God's purpose for his people. From the beginning, God teaches a basic generosity to be practiced within the confines of the nation Israel. Two key passages from Israel's constitution reveal this informed humaneness of God. The first deals with the institution of a Sabbath year:

> At the end of every seven years you must grant a remission. Now the nature of the remission is this: every creditor who holds the person of his neighbour in bond must grant him remission; he may not exact payment from his fellow or his brother once the latter appeals to Yahweh for remission. From a foreigner you may exact payment, but you must remit whatever claim you have on your brother. Let there be no poor among you then. For Yahweh will bless you in the land Yahweh your God gives you for your inheritance only if you pay careful attention to the voice of Yahweh your God, keeping and observing all these commandments that I enjoin on you today. If Yahweh your God blesses you as he promised, you will be creditors to many nations and debtors to none; you will rule over many nations and be ruled by none.
>
> Is there a poor man among you, one of your brothers, in any town of yours in the land that Yahweh your God is giving you? Do not harden your heart to close your hand against that poor brother of yours, but be open-handed with him and lend him enough for his

> needs. Do not allow this mean thought in your heart,
> "The seventh year, the year of remission is near," and
> look coldly on your poor brother and give him nothing;
> he could appeal against you to Yahweh and it would be
> sin for you. When you give to him, you must give with
> an open heart; for this Yahweh your God will bless you
> in all you do and in all your giving. Of course there will
> never cease to be poor in the land; I command you there-
> fore: Always be open-handed with your brother, and
> with anyone in your country who is in need and poor
> (Deut 15:1–11, JB).

Every seventh year was a "year of remission," when every debt would be forgiven and slaves, therefore, set free. In a broad sense, this year symbolized the kingdom of God. There is no slavery in God's kingdom; there is no indebtedness. While Israel was not the perfect earthly representation of the kingdom, her practices were meant to reflect the consummation—the new heavens and the new earth. So in Israel there was to be a restraint placed upon evils that ultimately, under the lordship of Jesus Christ, would not exist at all.

A system built upon slavery, a system built upon credit, is an evil system. So every seventh year all debts were to be forgiven, and the enslavement of people who would voluntarily sell themselves to creditors to work off their debt would become unnecessary. While this practice of observing the Sabbath year would not eradicate poverty, it would certainly go a long way toward restraining the polarization of rich and poor, creditor and debtor, master and slave.

There is in God's heart a wisdom whose beginning implications (even before we get to the Sermon on the Mount!) are radical enough for the Christian community. Will we Christians ever get around to observing the Sabbath? And the observance of the Sabbath as Deuteronomy defines it is still a giant step from the coming of Jesus and his establishment of God's kingdom.

Perhaps it should be pointed out that God indicates a connection between a credit system and a system of slavery. As long as the credit system flourishes as the basis of our economy, will not slavery (even though voluntary in some aspects) be the keystone of social "progress"? The practice of usury needs to be examined as perhaps the most exploitative and oppressive institution of our society, whereby the rich get richer and the poor get poorer. Loaning money at interest has become a respectable profession, but the banker and the slave trader are not-too-distant occupational cousins, I suspect.

In this Deuteronomy passage, we also see that God is interested in more than just restraining a system likely to be abused. He first tackles the root of the problem with some preventive medicine—the observance of the Sabbath year—then prescribes some further action for a society where the poor, despite God's ideal (Deut 15:4), will nevertheless continue to exist in the land. Not only must the creditors cancel debts owed them every seventh year, but everyone must at all times give freely to brother, needy, and poor in the land.

The Deuteronomy passage is revolutionary, but a similar passage in Leviticus goes beyond even its injunctions. Again the Sabbath year is discussed, coupled with the institution of a Jubilee Year—every fiftieth year, that is, the year following seven sets of seven years. The Jubilee Year is described as a year in which all land is returned to its original owner (Lev 25:23–28).

The land was originally divided up fairly among the families and tribes when Israel settled in the promised land, so this initial equality coupled with a built-in safeguard against the prolonged hoarding of property served to guarantee every citizen's right to own land. Land in Israel's agrarian society was the most precious possession, and therefore most apt to be the object of speculation and acquisition. The practice of owning inordinate amounts of land has, like banking, become honorable in our society, but it was restrained as an evil among the ancient people of God. We would do well as Christians to consider the implications for our own lives.

Leviticus 25:35–43 should not surprise us and needs no further comment:

> If your brother who is living with you falls on evil days and is unable to support himself with you, you must support him as you would a stranger or a guest, and he must continue to live with you. Do not make him work for

you, do not take interest from him; fear your God, and
let your brother live with you. You are not to lend him
money at interest, or give him food to make a profit out
of it. I am Yahweh your God who brought you out of the
land of Egypt to give you the land of Canaan and to be
your God.

If your brother falls on evil days when he is with you
and sells himself to you, you must not impose a slave's
work on him; he shall be like a hired man or a guest,
and shall work with you until the jubilee year. Then he
shall leave you, he and his children; he shall return to his
clan and regain possession of his ancestral property. For
they are my servants, these whom I have brought out of
Egypt, and they must not be sold like slaves. You must
not be a hard master to him, but you must fear your God
(Lev 25:35–43, JB).

The problem was not the private ownership of land. Everyone in
Israel, except the Levites, was to own land. The problem was (and
is) that if someone owns more than his or her share, then obviously
someone else has to do without. If we followed Israel's pattern, we
would redistribute our land every fifty years.

The problem is enslaving people, by taking advantage of their
immediate need in order to provide for the creditor's long-range
welfare. The evil genius of the system becomes evident when one
considers that a poor man may work twice as hard to buy something that a rich man may be able to afford, despite his idleness, by
taking advantage of someone else's toil. The rich man is not simply
putting his money to work; he is putting his "slaves" to work!

If these Old Testament injunctions were so important to the
life and welfare of the people of God, why are they not reestab-
lished or reaffirmed in the New Testament? Can we not justifiably
claim that Christ has freed us from our obligation to the law? My
answer to that question is that we are of course free from the law
if we are in Christ Jesus. But being "in" Christ means having the
mind of Christ, which cannot contradict the Old Testament revelation of the heart of God. God's revelation to Israel has been sur-
passed. I am not asking that the archaic institutions of the Sabbath

Year and the Jubilee Year be the ethical definition and standard for Christians. The celebration of the Lord's Supper is our institution. We need no other.

To ask a New Testament follower of Christ to give up his slaves, cancel his debts, and forsake his overabundance of land is like challenging an Eagle Scout to tie a square knot.

The examples of the Sabbath Year and the Jubilee Year are sufficient to illustrate an additional Old Testament principle that finds its consummation in the New Testament. We should not overlook the essence of celebration and release that is built into the heart of Hebrew life. The Sabbath Year was not to be feared by the people. Even those who owned the slaves were to rejoice at the formal opportunity to cancel the debts of those who were submissive to them.

How out of place it would have been for any of God's chosen ones to nurture the spirit of greed and acquisition, to set one's heart on material gain, but not because there was anything inherently evil about wealth. Indeed, the whole nation was to be wealthy! But man's genius was never to be the basic source of his welfare. The open hand of God was to be the root of Israel's prosperity. She was to be a great nation in every sense of the term (Gen 12:2–3) because her people were the children of Yahweh. They were to seek him, to know him, to depend upon him for daily bread and life. Seeking frantically or even casually after material things, in both testaments, is wrong because it is pagan; it denies the generous fatherhood of God.

The spirit of sharing was to be the norm within the nation of Israel. There was no necessity for special projects to feed the hungry in their midst. Sharing with the hungry was the law of the land.

> When you go into your neighbour's vineyard, you may eat your fill of grapes, as many as you wish, but you shall not put any in your vessel. When you go into your neighbour's standing grain, you may pluck the ears with your hand, but you shall not put a sickle to your neighbour's standing grain (Deut 23:25–26, JB).

The ideal that God projected for his people Israel might be summed up as follows: There was to be one class of people. There was to be no poverty, and wherever this ideal was not carried out there was to be an immediate generosity to alleviate the problem and a permanent institution (the Sabbath) to eradicate it. There was to be complete dependence upon God for material as well as spiritual blessing. Faithfulness was to issue in prosperity, a sign of God's blessing.

9. The Witness of the Prophets

SOME COMMENTATORS HAVE NOTED how well Israel observed these principles. John Bright points out in his *History of Israel*: "Judean towns of the late eighth century (some 600 years after the giving of the law) had a remarkable homogeneity of population, and yield few signs of extreme wealth or poverty. . . . Some evidences of a common prosperity may be observed."[1]

But by this time the northern kingdom had already fallen to Assyria and the disintegration of the south (Judah) had begun. Along with the military threat to the divided nation, its spiritual and material welfare was jeopardized. Spiritual apostasy was actually the root cause of all of Israel's national problems. As the people were captured and torn from the land flowing with milk and honey that God had given them, their role in God's plan began to change. For Israel to become a channel of blessing to all nations would require a national transition whose implications are still being discovered by the new Israel (the Christian church).

The comments of the prophets of the eighth century BC reveal the sorry decline of Israel's religious and moral life. The oppression and exploitation that God had so carefully tried to restrain became one visible sign of the waywardness of his flock. Therefore, prophesies Isaiah, "Yahweh calls to judgement the elders and the princes of his people: 'You are the ones who destroy the vineyard and conceal what you have stolen from the poor. By what right do

1. Bright, *A History of Israel*, 4th ed. (Louisville: Westminster John Knox, 2000), 260.

you crush my people and grind the faces of the poor?' It is the Lord Yahweh Sabaoth who speaks" (Isa 3:14–15, JB).

And again, "Woe to the legislators of infamous laws, to those who issue tyrannical decrees, who refuse justice to the unfortunate and cheat the poor among my people of their rights, who make widows their prey and rob the orphan" (Isa 10:1–2, JB).

The corruption and self-righteousness that follow upon oppression are cited by the prophet Micah, a contemporary of Isaiah:

> Now Listen to this, you princes of the House of Jacob, rulers of the House of Israel, you who loathe justice and pervert all that is right, you who build Zion with blood, Jerusalem with crime. Her princes pronounce their verdict for bribes, her priests take a fee for their rulings, her prophets make divinations for money. And yet they rely on Yahweh. They say, "Is not Yahweh in our midst? No evil is going to overtake us" (Mic 3:9–11, JB).

Perhaps Amos is most explicit in his statement of the harsh realities confronting the oppressive upper class:

> Listen to this word, you cows of Bashan living in the mountain of Samaria, oppressing the needy, crushing the poor . . . .The days are coming to you now when you will be dragged out with hooks, the very last of you with prongs . . . . Well then, since you have trampled on the poor man, extorting levies on his wheat—those houses you have built of dressed stone, you will never live in them; and those precious vineyards you have planted, you will never drink their wine" (Amos 4:1–2 and 5:11, JB).

In any discussion of materialism and the Old Testament, the practice of tithing is mentioned, often as if it were the only insight offered by the Hebrew tradition. I believe we have discovered a great deal of material more crucial to our present analysis than the concept of tithing. The tithe was instituted to support the Levites, whose work was to be the maintenance of the religious life of the people (Num 18:21–24). The affairs of the Tent of Meeting, later replaced by the temple, and of the extensive sacrificial system, were theirs to administer. They had a privileged leadership role in the nation's life, and the responsibility that accompanied their duties warranted that they receive their income from the offerings of the people. Therefore God decreed that the first 10 percent of a family's income (mostly in the form of grain and meat) be sacrificed to them as symbolic atonement for sin and as sustenance for God's special representatives, the Levites.

The sacrificial system has of course been fulfilled by Jesus Christ, and the role of the Levites is now obsolete, Christ being our high priest forever. The tithe cannot therefore be equated with modern-day church giving or charity. The tithe was not to be devoted to the care of the widow or the orphan. Missionary activity was not supported by the tithe. There is little theological support for 10 percent as being either a minimum or maximum level of giving, so I believe the tithe has only an indirect bearing on our quest for a contemporary concept of giving.

The grace of God given in the incarnation has catapulted us into a whole new reality where the tithe seems out of place. In the New Testament, our bodies are God's temple and, similarly, our whole lives are the sacrifice acceptable to God (1 Cor 6:19 and Rom 12:1).

10. The Transition Between the Testaments

ISRAEL WAS ORIGINALLY TO be a showcase nation. She was to attract her neighbors, by virtue of her material prosperity and other factors, to worship her God. Each nation was thought to have its own deity who was responsible for the national welfare. What actually happened, because Israel left her God, was national collapse. The nation that was to be the envy of its neighbors became a laughingstock. The master became a slave.

The channel-of-blessing role that God had from the beginning projected for his people was not to be thwarted, however. God cannot be kept from accomplishing his purposes by disobedience, even on a nationwide scale. And so toward the end of the Old Testament we glimpse a new covenant, a new arrangement whereby the people of God would indeed be the world's entrance to God's blessing and resources. That people of God was to be represented by an individual, a Messiah, and by his spiritual offspring, a new Israel. The old Israel would languish in exile and national disgrace to be finally redeemed at a future time. The new Israel would emerge as an entirely new humanity from the remnant of the old.

The exiled nation experienced a foretaste of God's punishment for their apostasy. But with every prophetic pronouncement of wrath there was an invitation to repentance and a promise of certain redemption. There would indeed be exaltation for God's people. The name of Yahweh could not forever be scorned. In the New Testament Paul cherishes the thought of the future exaltation of his people. In the Old Testament the prophets speak in ultimate terms of the kingdom that will some day be realized.

But what of the new Israel?

What is the present role of God's people? We who are God's disciples in the present will certainly share in a future exaltation with our ancestors in the faith. But the role God has for us is the reversal of the role God initially envisioned for the descendants of Abraham. The Old Testament prophets speak of the suffering servant as both an individual and a nation, a personal Messiah and a humiliated body of believers. God's purpose has not changed. The Christ was slain from the foundation of the world. The daughters and sons of God were destined from the beginning to be a servant race. Redemption would be discovered through ordeal and suffering. Blessing would be conveyed through a despised remnant. Reconciliation would come through the cross. God would become flesh, would identify with humanity, and would become a curse for us.

In the same way that the Son was sent into the world, so would he send his followers. In the power of the Holy Spirit they too would become the wretched of the earth. This is what it means to accept the cross for one's life—to become a follower of the "Way." It is a way that no human could have devised. It is not natural for any of us to accept the wisdom of God.

Second Isaiah, probably written by a postexilic prophet, embodies most of the prediction of the role reversal that would transform the future members of the house of David. Isaiah 40–66 articulates the massive transition from the Old Testament to the New. Most of us have not made the transition. The church has certainly become a fish out of water, a stranger to God's purpose, striving for a secular success and acceptance that is not to be ours in this life. As we understand who Jesus is, as we behold his glory, then we understand the transition, and we understand who we are to be.

There is a staggering difference between the Old and the New. Jesus is a surprise, coming to us from the cradle, fasting in the wilderness, despised and rejected, the crucified one. Is this the chosen one of God? Is this the Lion of the tribe of Judah? Is this God visiting salvation and blessing upon his people?

The Jews of his day could not understand Jesus. He was certainly not the Messiah they had expected. The disciples could not come to grips with his passion; their minds boggled at the thought of God's anointed being the world's servant-victim.

The modern church and many of its related nondenominational ministries have declared the way of the cross to be a hoax. None of us are conditioned to accept a crucified God and the manner of life that flows from the cross. May God's Spirit prepare us for the New Testament!

For the New Testament can teach us nothing about materialism until it teaches us about the new creation, about who the people of God are. When we understand that we are the body of Christ, when we permit the heart of God as revealed in the Old Testament to generate the mind of Christ in the New Testament and in our lives, then we will know and begin to implement the answers to our questions about discipleship.

The outward evidence of Israel's faithfulness was to be her greatness among the nations. In the New Testament, there is again to be an outward evidence of faithfulness. We are to be the poor and oppressed of the world. The life of Jesus Christ and his commandment to us speak powerfully of the New Testament mark of a Christian: "I give you a new commandment: love one another; just as I have loved you, you also must love one another. By this love you have for one another, everyone will know that you are my disciples" (John 13:34–35, JB).

The Israelites were to love one another, as we have already seen. But their love was approximate and conditional. God's love for us in Jesus Christ is total and unconditional. The Israelites loved their fellow Israelites, but they were under no obligation to love foreigners or their enemies. As we make the transition between the Old Testament and the New, it is important for us to understand that we are entering a new era, and we are subject to a new commandment: to love our enemies as well as our friends to the point of giving them our lives. This is precisely how God has loved us.

We have touched on many aspects of Old Testament truth. We have made the point that the Old prepares us for the New as much as possible. The truth of the incarnation, God becoming flesh, is best understood when we see it as the culmination of God's historic plan for humanity. We enter into God's plan freely, and yet, in a seeming paradox, behind our freedom of choice is the irresistible flow of God's purpose. God's plan from the beginning was that we would reflect his glory—that we would be his people. When sin entered the world it meant that the victory would be delayed, but not denied. When Israel failed to be the nation that God intended it to be, when it followed its free choice to disobedience and exile, then God's plan (at least from our finite perspective) took a final dramatic turn.

The blessing in the Old Testament was to rest with a nation that would eventually channel it to all nations. The greatness and prosperity of that nation were to be signs of God's favor upon it. Israel was to go forth as a bold, compelling light to the Gentiles. The pagan nations would be overwhelmed by the glory of Israel and would seek her God.

But Israel at the close of the Old Testament is far from glory. Stripped of her national sovereignty, her allegiance to Yahweh dissipated in a maze of corruption and idolatry, she is defeated and defenseless.

11. INFINITE GRACE

GOD IS NOT TO be denied. From weakness and obscurity Israel brings forth a savior, a Messiah. From his appearance and circumstance, no one would guess that he is the chosen one of God, an only begotten Son. Upon him and him alone rests the inheritance, the blessing. To speak of Jesus is, in the providence of God's plan, to speak of honor, glory, vindication, and abundance.

The concept of Sabbath, of Jubilee, of the kingdom of God, has become flesh. The blessing has become a person, and history's onslaught will never be able to separate the blessing from the person, the gift from the giver. Jesus does not pass the blessing on to us, as if it were a property, an object. Rather, he gives us himself, his body. Only as we participate in his person do we share in the blessing of the Father. The most profound New Testament truth, then, is not that Jesus is an example to be admired or imitated. He is a body to be entered. The sacraments, the symbols of relationship, mean that we are baptized into his body and we partake of his flesh. And this is blessing!

To ask the question, "Who is Jesus?" is to ask "What is the church?" or "Who am I?" The incarnation continues in us. Even though we are not the historic Messiah, the head of the body, the firstfruits, we nevertheless are Christ made visible to the world, the descendants of the Messiah, the new humanity. Our lives are continuous with the life of Christ. We are transformed into his nature by his Holy Spirit.

III—THE CHRISTIAN AND MATERIALISM

All this is important background if the New Testament concept of materialism is to make sense to us. For now that the blessing is personified, man's quest is focused on Jesus. "All I want," says Paul, "is to know Christ and the power of his resurrection and to share his sufferings by reproducing the pattern of his death" (Phil 3:10, JB). To know him is blessing, to be apart from him is curse. There is no meaning apart from him. Nothing is good apart from him. He is the "good." And so it is meaningless to ask, "Should I seek riches or should I seek poverty?" as if either represented inherent blessing or inherent curse.

We seek Jesus.

What does it mean for our everyday lives to seek Jesus, the Christ, to know him? Can we say that in seeking Christ we have also found, as a by-product of relationship with him, wealth? Can we say that the blessing of knowing Christ in a spiritual sense has issued in a material abundance? No! Not the Christ of the New Testament, the real Christ. To know Christ in today's world and in this life is to experience what Christ experienced in his world and in his earthly life. We must know the crucified Christ—he is the Christ available to us now—in order to know the resurrected Christ, who waits for us in the wings of history.

Faith is to believe so deeply that humiliation leads to exaltation, disgrace issues in glory, and death gives way to life, that we are willing to undergo humiliation, disgrace, and death for Christ's sake. God will check us on our belief. He will make us live it out. History will bring the cup of suffering to our lips. If our lives remain untested, it is not because history has been kind to us, it is because we have sidestepped the call to discipleship. Faith in a vacuum is no faith. God does not ask us to have faith just in case the rainy days come our way. Life in this century *is* a rainy day. Some of us ought to go outside our own little secure niche and see what Jesus saw. We don't need to have a persecution complex in order to pick up our cross, we need to have a reality complex.

Early in his ministry, Jesus speaks to his disciples. They have each made some dramatic break with their customary way of life and have pledged themselves to this man Jesus. But they know little about what is in store for them. They know enough to attach some religious significance to their new venture. What they know of blessing comes from their common Jewish heritage: The glory days of Israel under David and Solomon have been the blessed golden years of military conquest, national honor, and economic prosperity. Israel awaits a return of "David" to the throne and a rebirth of eternal glory. Is this Jesus, despite his small beginnings, perhaps the one to lead them and the people of God to blessing? Jesus answers their unspoken questions with a strange affirmative:

> Blessed are you poor, for yours is the kingdom of God.
>
> Blessed are you that hunger now, for you shall be satisfied.
>
> Blessed are you that weep now, for you shall laugh.
>
> Blessed are you when men hate you, and when they exclude you and revile you, and cast out your name as evil, on account of the Son of man!
>
> Rejoice in that day, and leap for joy, for behold, your reward is great in heaven; for so their fathers did to the prophets (Luke 6:20–23, RSV).

Jesus is describing his own life, to be shared by them, in the present and in the future. The disciples are to realize later that they cannot enter the future glory (the kingdom, the inheritance, the comfort, and so on) without participating in the present shame. They will also realize that they cannot enter fully into the present without a vital belief in the future. The blessing, like the treasure hidden in the field, lies buried in the dirt. Who will persevere to find it? Who will consider with Paul that "the sufferings of this present time are not worth comparing with the glory that is to be revealed to us" (Rom 8:18, RSV)?

To make the definition of the Christian ethic even more clear, Jesus describes the anti-Christian ethic:

> But woe to you that are rich, for you have received your consolation.
>
> Woe to you that are full now, for you shall hunger.

> Woe to you that laugh now, for you shall mourn and
> weep.
>
> Woe to you, when all men speak well of you, for so their
> fathers did to the false prophets (Luke 6:24–26, RSV).

The kingdom has come in Jesus Christ, and to the extent that he
rules within us, the kingdom is within us (Luke 17:21). But the
kingdom is also future, in the sense that we pray for the kingdom
to come to the world as a whole (Matt 6:10). We therefore wait for
Christ's return, when he will establish his perfect reign of peace,
which is already begun in us.

God in Christ has not become ascetic. He has not reversed
his Old Testament concern to shower material blessings upon his
people. The earth is still the Lord's and the fullness thereof. All that
he has made, including man's creative genius and its benefits, is
good. But the disobedience of Israel has postponed the consummation of the kingdom (again only from our human standpoint) until
the ordeal of crucifixion and the sufferings of Christ are completed.
This is the work that the church is called upon to finish. Our role is
that of the suffering servant, reconciling the world to God.

It is really an improper question to ask, "Is it wrong to be
wealthy?" There is no inherent rightness or wrongness to wealth.
The answer hinges upon our life situation. If we are outside the
resurrected state, which we are until the return of Christ (1 Cor
15:35–53), it is wrong to have wealth.

The modern institutional church is thus a doctrinal miscar-
riage, much like someone who laughs at funerals and weeps at
births. We are out of step with the God of history, and thus subject
to the indictment of Jesus: "They are like children sitting in the
market place and calling to one another, 'We piped to you, and you
did not dance; we wailed, and you did not weep'" (Luke 7:32, RSV).

A serious concern we must deal with is expressed by the
question, "Why?" Why has God denied us material blessing in
this age? We have already implied some answers that show that
God is not being mean to us. Rather, he wants us to have faith in
our future vindication, to hunger and thirst for it, and to believe

even though we have not seen. He wants us to know the source of blessing—himself.

The prophet Malachi speaks of God's cursing the very blessings that he had previously given Israel (Mal 2:2), because she rejoiced in the gift rather than the Giver. Would we not do the same? We are so prone to take God for granted. He wants us to desperately seek him and his goodness and not to accept any imitation that the world may offer. I have often said in partial jest, "Poor people are happy because all they have is each other." Of course, rich people have each other too, but things so often get in the way of personal relationships—the deeper source of joy. But all of these answers represent only side aspects of the wisdom of God. The real core reason discipleship and poverty go hand in hand is because of the depth of compassion revealed in the life of Jesus. Compassion is what makes vulnerability, emptiness, and poverty inevitable.

We glimpse the nature of God in the Old Testament, but we feast upon the fullness of his nature in the incarnation. "For God so loved the world, that he gave . . ." (John 3:16, RSV). In response to what the Hebrews knew of their national (to their way of thinking) deity, they were to be generous with one another. In response to God's grace, they were to care for each other, protect each other's rights to land and livelihood, and especially open their hearts to the unfortunate among them. But God's definition of compassion is not complete until he sends his Son to die on the cross.

This is infinite grace—so infinite, in fact, that it trumps our disobedience and our free will. God would not be God if his purpose for us were stymied by our disobedience and our free will! We all succumb to the grace of God—"That at the name of Jesus every knee should bow, in heaven and on earth and under the earth, and every tongue confess that Jesus Christ is Lord, to the glory of God the Father" (Phil 2:10–11, RSV).

What can be an appropriate response on our part to a God who gave himself for us without reservation while we were still his enemies? Can we love only our own and say that we have the mind of Christ? Can we forgive seven times and say that we have fulfilled the law? Can we restrict our giving to a tithe? We are not concerned here about earning the grace of God, as if giving were a means to an end. Rather, we are groping to respond to an end that has already been accomplished, to a grace that has already been given.

Before we give anything, should we not ask the question: "Does the one whom I seek to help deserve my help?" Did we deserve God's Son? Should we not at least ask: "What will he do with my gift? Will he use it wisely?" What did we do with God's Son? Have we used the gifts of God wisely? So you readily see that there can be no conditions to our giving according to whether the recipient is deserving or undeserving, friend or enemy. Even among pagans there is a generosity among friends. Nor can we withhold our gifts until we have assurances that they will be well-received and used properly. This is not to say that we ought to give blindly. We ought always be guided by the Spirit of God. But we cannot set any absolute conditions upon our giving. If God had been guided by the world's wisdom, who among us would be redeemed?

Our fulfillment is not ultimately realized in helping other people. Our fulfillment is primarily found in identifying with the poverty of Christ who had no place of his own to lay his head in life or in death. Our giving of course goes far beyond the material, but no New Testament student can deny the material poverty of Christ and the early church.

The New Testament's direct teaching on materialism represents an overwhelming bulk of material that ought to stop us in our tracks and turn the church around 180 degrees. Many will be dismayed to find an alarming consistency as we consider the example and teaching of Jesus, and the response of the New Testament church. Scripture will be cited in these areas and explained to show how it confirms the biblical framework that has already been laid.

The core institution of the New Testament and of our lives is the Lord's Supper. It is referred to as a sacrament, that is, a symbol of reality—an outward visible sign of an inward spiritual state. Outwardly, we eat the "body" and drink the "blood" of Jesus. Inwardly, we become one with him. The Lord's Supper is really all that needs to be said about materialism, if we only understood its implications. For when we share the life of Jesus, when we are instilled with his mind, we say to the world that we are now broken, that our blood is now spilt. We give ourselves to the world. Does anyone among us think that he or she can escape the consequences of such a commitment?

When Paul speaks of the Lord's Supper in 1 Corinthians 11:17–34, he uses the words of Jesus: "This is my body, which for you (is) being broken." The breaking of the bread symbolizes the impoverishment of the body. "My life is given over for your use," Jesus is saying. "I am consecrated to you." As Jesus did for his enemies, we are to do for ours. "Do this in remembrance of me." Do what? Not just go through a ritual! But become broken as we take into ourselves the broken Christ. It is not so much that we are acting upon him, by eating his body; he is acting upon us, by transforming us into the new humanity, the poured-out human resources of God. We do not proclaim the Lord's death by kneeling at a communion rail. That is only a symbol, a sacrament. We proclaim the Lord's death by dying. The whole rationale for our new existence is the Lord's death. We are to be in the process of dying until he comes. When he comes again it will not be to die, but to reign as Lord of the realized kingdom. Then we will no longer take communion as a sacrament. Who needs a memorial service, a symbol of reality, when the one being remembered is present, when the reality is overwhelmingly apparent?

The church thinks Christ has already arrived, the second time, and that we no longer need to proclaim his death. The world is just peachy keen. And if we were to offer ourselves to the world as living sacrifices, who would there be to claim us and crucify us? "Is everybody happy?" "Yes!" Then there is no need for reconciling God to man. It is already done. We are all resurrected, and the world has become a good garden of Eden once again!

I sense the deep sarcasm of Paul when he wrote to the Corinthian church:

> Already you are filled! Already you have become rich!
> Without us you have become kings! And would that you
> did reign, so that we might share the rule with you! For I
> think that God has exhibited us as apostles as last of all,

> like men sentenced to death: because we have become a
> spectacle to the world, to angels and to men. We are fools
> for Christ's sake, but you are wise in Christ. We are weak,
> but you are strong. You are held in honor, but we are ill-
> clad and buffeted and homeless, and we labor, working
> with our own hands. When reviled, we bless: when per-
> secuted, we endure; when slandered, we try to conciliate;
> we have become, and are now, as the refuse of the world,
> the offscouring of all things (1 Cor 4:8–13, RSV).

You see, Paul knew what it meant to celebrate the Lord's Supper. That is why he warned so sternly those who would come casually to the Lord's table "without discerning the body," that is, without understanding the brokenness.

Jesus spoke to the multitudes about counting the cost of following him (Luke 14:25–33). He spoke not only of the initial cost, but of the ultimate cost—if we are to finish "building the tower." We must give up everything, not in one impulsive act, but in one continuous act of giving, with emptiness as our goal.

I take Jesus seriously at this point. I take the example of his life seriously. "Poverty" is not really a difficult word to understand. The early church had a saying: "You are to let your offering sweat in the palm of your hand until you know for whom it is intended." I believe that statement, though not authoritative for us in the sense the Bible is, can be squared with the New Testament. I believe Jesus waited for the direction of the Spirit. He enjoyed some feasting along the way; he kept his seamless robe until the end. But he was in the process of aggressively becoming poor. There is no mechanical blueprint to follow to arrive at the cross. Our response to Jesus is not blind or irrational. It is an intelligent faith that the last shall be first, and the first last (Mark 9:35), that the hungry are being filled with good things and the rich sent away empty (Luke 1:52–54), and that the greatest in God's eyes must be the least and the servant of all (Matt 23:11).

These are the concepts we must believe and follow. Just as the mind of the world draws its adherents to the pursuit of primacy,

Jesus draws his followers to the cross. The quest for obscurity and emptiness fills our lives.

It is clear in this parable of the man building the tower and of the king going to war that Jesus is speaking of this quest to a multitude of people (Luke 14:25). This group was the usual random crowd that included everyone from the curious to the deeply committed. He spoke to all of them of a process that would lead them to poverty. It is the process of discipleship.

Poverty—the renunciation of all things—is to be the norm and the goal of the Christian experience. Christ did not become poor in a day. But at the beginning of the battle, he counted the ultimate cost, and he embraced the consequences. So must we all. The Greek says literally: "Thus therefore everyone of you who does not take leave of all that he possesses cannot be my disciple" (Luke 14:33). How should we Christians deal with this passage?

I do know something of how the early church responded: "And all who believed were together and had all things in common; and they sold their possessions and goods and distributed them to all, as any had need" (Acts 2:44–45, RSV).

It is of course unfortunate that the Jerusalem church as it emerged in those days immediately following Pentecost did not have the wisdom of those skilled theologians or the common sense of those bold preachers of the Word who bless us today with their interpretation of this mystical Greek language. For of course the suffering and persecution that Jesus holds out to us are to be taken quite figuratively, and no one really expects the Christian in our day to pay anything more than a symbolic nominal portion of the original cost of discipleship. I will not question the salvation of the well-intentioned faithful—pastors, professors, and lay people—who lead the church. I would only suggest that if God interprets the "glory that will one day be revealed" as casually as we interpret the "suffering of this present day," then we might all be disappointed.

Jesus was well within the law when he went through the grain fields with his hungry band and ate freely of the produce. (Matt 12:1–8, cf. Deut 23:24–25). Even the Pharisees did not criticize him for "stealing." Their only argument was that he was desecrating the Sabbath day by "harvesting." But the real meaning of the Sabbath, which they overlooked, was that everyone should have his needs met. In response to the Pharisees Jesus said, "The Son of man is lord of the sabbath" (Matt 12:8, RSV).

The earliest creed of the Christian community was "Jesus is Lord." When we say "Jesus is Lord" are we not also saying "All our needs are met in him"? Are not the two statements identical? Else what does it mean to say "Jesus is Lord"?

When we say "Jesus is Lord" we are saying that he controls us and, ultimately, the affairs of men and women. It may appear that injustice is the norm, that fate is lord, that greed has won the day. But no matter how overwhelming the sense of despair that confronts us existentially, we as Christians bear witness to an ultimate reality that is more overwhelming still. This reality of God's kingdom has swept us into the flow of history as its early-bird ambassadors to make a startling announcement to the world: justice reigns, kindness holds sway, the blind see, mercy flows forth. And our lives are chosen by God to give evidence of the quality of the new creation.

Our message is utterly supernatural, generated by the historic resurrection and exaltation of our Messiah, rooted in the fact that Jesus Christ is Lord. When his lordship grips our lives, the kingdom of God is born within us, and we are freed to become servants to the world that will one day fully experience his kingdom. We are free to become poor, not because there is some inherent goodness in poverty, but because we poor possess the kingdom; and we are free to mourn, not because there is some secret exhilaration in gloominess, but because the Comforter wipes away every tear; and we are free, indeed compelled, to forego all right to our lives and our possessions, because all our needs are met in him, because Jesus Christ is Lord.

This point is so crucial to the Christian ethic, perhaps it needs further illustration. Let us look for a moment at the life of Christ. A three-year ministry seemingly ends at the cross. The disciples flee for their own lives. The crowds slander the suffering criminal. Jesus is abandoned by God the Father. All four Gospels record other various details of his agony. Human events have brought Jesus to the end of a ministry that at times appeared to be full of hope for mankind. But men have passed a negative judgment upon his life and its promise. Yet as Jesus breathes his last, there is a hint of another judgment, an ultimate verdict. The judgment of God intervenes and overturns the decision of Rome, of the Sanhedrin, and of you and me. The sky turns black, a pagan soldier whispers an embryonic testimony: "In truth, this man was a son of God" (Mark 15:39, JB). God raises him from the dead. And the exaltation of Christ has begun.

With the ultimate verdict of God rendered, it becomes our lot to ratify that verdict with our own lives as we await the full realization of the kingdom in history. We are middle men and middle women, living in the tension between the first and second comings of Christ—knowing the fact of his lordship, yearning to have history work out its inherent confirmation of the Truth: the valleys shall be lifted up, the mountains and hills made low (Isa 40:1); the first shall be last, and the last first (Mark 9:35); justice will roll down like waters, and mercy like an ever-flowing stream (Amos 5:24); and every knee shall bow and every tongue confess that Jesus Christ is Lord. (Phil 2:10–11).

The life and teachings of Jesus are vindicated in the resurrection, and if we don't live out his life and teachings, then we plainly don't believe his resurrection. Our lives, much more decisively than our words, either proclaim or deny Jesus and his kingdom. It is not enough to nurture a sentimental yearning for the days of yore when Jesus walked beside the sea or to cherish the memory of his magic words. The question is, have we become poor with him? Have we emptied ourselves as he did? Have we picked up our cross? Have we permitted the little children to come to us? Have we fed the hungry? Have we touched the lepers of our world?

The answers to these questions are the context for our proclamation and the confirmation of our faith. The more we share his suffering, the more clearly and loudly we proclaim his lordship. The joyous and compassionate life of physical and spiritual poverty is fundamental for both discipleship and evangelism.

Do we not see that it is impossible for a rich man to say to a poor man, "Jesus is Lord"? If the rich man truly believed it, his confidence in a future exaltation would permit him to become poor that others might be rich, and his compassion for his sisters and brothers would compel him to do just that. When Jesus says your sins are forgiven, he also says, indeed he must say, pick up your bed and walk (Matt 9:6). Do we not weep to know that a rich church has nothing redemptive to say to the dispossessed?

I believe that Christ went to both worlds—the rich and the poor—with his message of peace, and perhaps the best example of his approach to the rich is the story of the rich young ruler. I wrote earlier that the believer's compassion and his poverty go hand in hand. This passage (Matt 19:16–30) shows the biblical basis for such a belief.

In response to the ruler's question about salvation, Jesus instructs him to keep the commandments, and he gives him a sample list ending with the commandment to love neighbor as self. It is clear that the young man loved himself, and he did so in rather concrete ways. He had provided for himself. He had amassed security for himself. He did not just glibly and conceptually say, "I love you, Self."

But what about his love for his neighbor? It is commendable that the man took care of himself. It is commendable that he is also able to express at least a sentiment of love for his neighbor. But the issue over which he loses his fellowship with Christ is the issue of whether he loves his neighbor as he loves himself. To make it apparent that the man really hasn't observed this supreme commandment, Jesus repeats the command in another form. He says, "Go, sell what you possess and give it to the poor." This is only a more specific way of saying, "Love your neighbor as yourself." The double standard of the rich young ruler (and the rich old church) now emerges for all to see. We have one standard for loving ourselves: we love ourselves concretely. The evidence of our love for ourselves would stand up in any court of law. But our love for our neighbor is subjective and symbolic. The evidence is all hearsay. "I hear what you say," says Jesus. "Now let's see you do it." His great possessions are proof that the rich young ruler loves himself. The fact that he will not part with them is proof that he does not love his neighbor. And that is why it is hard for a rich man to get into the kingdom of heaven, not because wealth is not allowed in heaven, but because cruelty is not allowed. And wealth in this day, when the poor are all about (Matt 26:11) is the surest sign that neighbors (including enemies) have not been loved.

Even wealthy persons, at least the ones I know and love, would admit that if they gave to everyone who asked they would quickly become poor. Yet that is precisely what Jesus asks all of his followers, not just the rich young ruler, when he says, "Give to him who begs from you, and do not refuse him who would borrow from you" (Matt 5:42, RSV) and "of him who takes away your goods do not ask them again" (Luke 6:30, RSV) and "Sell your possessions and give alms" (Luke 12:33, RSV). In fact, the Christian should not wait to be asked. "But if anyone has the world's goods and sees his brother in need, yet closes his heart against him, how does God's love abide in him? Little children, let us not love in word or speech but in deed and in truth" (1 John 3:17–18, RSV).

A parable that has an important bearing on our subject is the account of the kingdom being likened to the treasure hidden in the field and the pearl of great price (Matt 13:44–46). In both cases the man "sells everything he owns" in order to possess the kingdom. There is something about the kingdom that demands a happy abandonment of this world's values and goods. The kingdom is an all-consuming passion. There is no eating our cake (in this world) and having it, too (in the world to come).

The story of the rich man and Lazarus (Luke 16:19–31) seems also to portray a situation that I believe has a clear lesson for us. Riches in this life mean torment in the life to come. Poverty in this life means the kingdom. It is as if Jesus had no regard for a man's faith, only for his circumstances. I am not saying that is true, I am only saying that there is a body of Old and New Testament material that can reasonably be held to support that interpretation. What the Scripture envisions when it pictures the valleys being lifted up and the mountains made low (without any apparent regard for faith or lack of faith) is the end time when the Christian community will indeed be the visibly oppressed and the pagan world will hold the upper hand. The servant-victim role for the church is a working out of historical certainties. Each of our lives, if we are faithful, represents a microcosm of this process.

In other words, the time is coming when the church will be a fellowship of beggars and the antichrist will be a community of wealth and power. When the polarization is complete, the tribulation of the church will be ended by the triumphant return of Christ. The question we must answer is whether we will cooperate with the flow of history by permitting our faith to lead us into oppression, or whether we will struggle in vain to unite God and mammon. Do we understand the Christian philosophy of history as personified by the rich man and Lazarus?

Rightly understood, both our faith and our appreciation of human destiny lead us to the cross. For a long time we have naively accepted the moral neutrality of wealth and power. We have even in the name of our faith sought positions of wealth and power so that we might influence events for the sake of Christ. But earthly wealth and power belong to the prince of this world, who is Satan. When we use his weapons, we become his pawns. Our true power is discovered in weakness (2 Cor 12:9–10). And weakness, to the point of crucifixion, is our destiny.

There is a deep joy that marks our steps toward the cross, mingled with reluctance because we know that the suffering will be real, and if there were another way, an easier ordeal, that this cup might pass from us, we would readily accept a stay of our execution. But history will not relent; the wisdom of the Father is higher than our wisdom. And so for the joy that is set before us we endure the cross as a way of life. And we discover the blessing of the kingdom of God that comes to the poor, literally the *ptochoi*, the beggars, of both Matthew 5:3 and Luke 6:20.

So let us unburden ourselves of the notion that there is a benign wealth that can be tolerated in our midst. There are some who say that wealth has just come their way. They haven't lusted after it or connived or exploited to achieve it. The attainment of wealth can be excused as a temporary station in life, perhaps as a real blessing of God, who clearly has the capacity to reward faith with wealth (cf. Job, and in the New Testament, 2 Corinthians 9:8–11, Mark 10:30). Paul himself says that he knows how to be wealthy (Phil 4:12). Jesus enjoyed some luxurious moments (Matt 26:6–13). But such a blessing is a dangerous one and an unusual one.

But what about wealth that does come to a Christian either by pure hard work or by inheritance? I believe we are permitted to receive such wealth (with fear and trembling!). But we are not permitted to store it up or accumulate it for purposes of earthly security, and surely if we follow even the mild advice of Paul in 1 Timothy 6:17–19, we will not retain our wealth for long. We are to be compassionate as our Father is compassionate (Luke 6:36). Certainly that precludes the maintenance of wealth.

The wealthy Christian and those of us who elevate him or her to a position of leadership have for a long time been easily familiar with the verse from 1 Timothy 6:10—"The love of money is the root of all evils" (RSV). We have quickly pointed out that it is not money, but the love of money, that is so demeaning. Here we make at least one and possibly two incorrect assumptions. We assume that a man can gain money without lusting for it. But in a world where competition for the dollar is becoming more ruthless, it becomes more and more difficult to become rich without making money and position the idols of our lives. Secondly, and more significantly, in a world where legitimate basic need is increasingly evident, lust is an absolute prerequisite for the prolonged enjoyment of wealth or security.

Another verse that gives false comfort to the rich is Matthew's version of the first beatitude: "Blessed are the poor in spirit" (Matt 5:3, RSV). The fact that Luke records simply, "Blessed are you poor" (Luke 6:20, RSV) is conveniently overlooked. I believe that both statements were made by Jesus on numerous occasions. Of course, you can be poor without being poor in spirit. Materialism is a sin in the ghetto as well as in the suburb. Those who have nothing may be just as greedy for things as the affluent. But the important fact is that you cannot be poor in spirit without that spirit issuing in a giving of self to the point of outward poverty.

Compassion and wealth will create such a tension in a person's life that they cannot coexist for very long. "You cannot serve God and mammon" (Matt 6:24, RSV). Either a person has to pass by on the other side, as the priest and the Levite did in the story of the Good Samaritan (Luke 10:29–37), or else give himself and his possessions as he encounters human need. The timetable for becoming poor is worked out in our daily encounters with humanity.

One of our challenges, therefore, and perhaps for many of us the most immediate, is the challenge to become friends with the oppressed. Of course, there are organizations that channel funds to the poor, and they are worthy of our intelligent support. There are also projects that may have good claim on our time and that may for awhile bring us into a different world. But eventually we must be drawn into a more intimate and continuous contact that is conducive to sharing ourselves with the less fortunate as equals. Gradually perhaps, but inevitably, we must step into the moccasins of a brother or walk a mile in the shoes of a sister who hungers and thirsts for a righteousness that we have taken for granted. We only degrade people if we become a "Santa Claus" to them.

There is no substitute for the logic of the incarnation, which demands that we "pitch our tent" among the oppressed just as Jesus dwelt among us. We must ask God for a compassionate heart and for eyes open to human need. We must ask God for the creativity and the wisdom that will translate our vulnerability into blessing—blessing for those who sense the love of God in our giving of ourselves, and blessing for us who sense the inner companionship of Christ as we undergo his crucifixion.

We go to the oppressed and we become one with them because that is where we find Christ in a unique and redemptive way. The import of Matthew 25:31–46 is that Christ is in our world as one who is hungry, thirsty, a stranger, naked, sick, imprisoned. We must seek him out and share with him whatever we have of food, drink, friendship, clothing, health, and freedom. This is the concrete opportunity that beckons each one of us to lose life . . . and find it.

12. The Spirit of the Early Church

THERE WERE A FEW rich people mentioned with kindness in the New Testament. Joseph of Arimathea, the best example, was a respected member of the Sanhedrin, waiting more sincerely than most for the kingdom of God, and a secret follower of Jesus who took the body and laid it in his own tomb (Mark 15:43, John 19:38). One wonders what became of Joseph. Did he ever openly declare himself? Did he sell all his possessions along with other early Christians? I don't want to detract from the nobility of Joseph's bold act. He, along with that other secret would-be follower Nicodemus, certainly behaved more commendably during the hour of crisis than the disciples. But I think the disciples had a great deal to teach Joseph. They had left everything to follow Jesus (Mark 10:28).

We make beautiful monuments to God, but we have denied countless cups of cold water in order to do so (Matt 10:42). We build monuments to our own lifeless religion. We, as individual Christians and as a corporate body, indict ourselves by laying up treasures on earth (Matt 6:19). If only the wealthy were secret followers, like Joseph, the credibility of Christianity among the oppressed of the world would skyrocket.

The presence of a few rich people within the early church, perhaps including Lydia (Acts 16:14, 15, 40) and other leading women (Acts 17:4), deserves mention chiefly because these people were the exception rather than the rule. The basic nature of the fellowship was not altered by their inclusion. Of course we only know of Joseph as a secret follower before the impact of the resurrection, and we only know of Lydia at the time of her conversion. Either Joseph and Lydia and their like changed their lifestyles or they risked great discomfort—the discomfort of being rich among the poor and the discomfort of hearing the scathing denunciations of wealth and warning to the rich quoted from Jesus and the apostles (notably Luke 6:24–26, and Jas 5:1–6; also Heb 13:5, Rev 3:17, and 1 Tim 3:3 and 6:8–10, 17–19).

There are numerous passages to support the contention that the early church was poor. Paul speaks of the Corinthians:

> Not many of you were wise according to worldly standards, not many were powerful, not many were of noble birth; but God chose what is foolish in the world to shame the wise, God chose what is weak in the world to shame the strong, God chose what is low and despised in the world, even things that are not, to bring to nothing things that are (1 Cor 1:26–28, RSV).

James's assessment is more pointed: "Has not God chosen those who are poor in the world to be rich in faith and heirs of the kingdom which he has promised to those who love him?" (Jas 2:5, RSV). The only one of the seven churches addressed in the book of Revelation to receive a full commendation is the church at Smyrna, to whom John writes, "I know your tribulation and your poverty" (Rev 2:9, RSV). Paul says he was taken for a pauper (2 Cor 6:10) and frequently cites the hunger that he undergoes for the sake of the gospel (2 Cor 6:5, 11:27, and Phil 4:12).

The members of the Jerusalem church, cited earlier in the Acts 2:44–45 and 4:33–35 passages, contributed all their possessions to a common pot shortly after they came together on the day of Pentecost. Later in its history the Jerusalem congregation found itself in great material need, apparently as a result of persecution and perhaps also because of their earlier practice. Paul cites their need as a glorious opportunity for other parts of the body to help the saints in Jerusalem (1 Cor 16:1–4, 2 Cor 8:1—9:15). Some might say that the Jerusalem fellowship had gone too far in their economic program. But Paul points out to the Corinthians that the body is meant to be interdependent. Need for either the material or the spiritual should not be a source of shame among the saints; nor should the supplying of that need be a source of pride.

The church was not to be an idle church. "If any one will not work, let him not eat" (2 Thess 3:10, RSV). But it was to be a continuously giving church, contributing to the needs of the saints and feeding the enemy as well (Rom 12:13, 20), joyfully accepting the plundering of its property in times of persecution (Heb 10:34), and eager to remember the poor (Matt 26:9 and Gal 2:10) and the widows (Acts 6:1–6).

13. A Summary and a Challenge

Who among us is worthy to share in the death of Jesus (2 Cor 4:10) and to follow in the tradition of the early church? We have an overwhelming task before us, yet one that can begin simply and quickly. We know the foolishness of building bigger barns to accommodate our wealth (Luke 12:13–21). We know the wisdom of the widow who contributed all she had (Mark 12:41–44). I suppose more could be said, but I can't think of another input that could make the mandate of Scripture any clearer. Becoming poor out of compassion for those we can help and out of a burning desire to know Christ is a goal we all must pursue.

I trust that no one has passed over quickly the New Testament material that I have cited. Everything that I have written stands or falls on the New Testament witness. I would not want to convince you with cleverness or emotional appeal, nor would I want you to sidestep the heart of God, the mind of Christ, by finding some questionable rationale for the status quo in your life. The strands of Scripture that I have brought together from the Gospels and the letters form the ethical and doctrinal basis of the church, and they are consistent in their teaching. They are not isolated verses. They are part of a fabric of thought that underlies the very nature of the body of Christ.

The body of Christ was never meant to be exalted in this life. Understand who Jesus is. He is a servant. He is a man of sorrows. He is scorned and rejected by men. And the church that is his offspring is to be a corporate servant to the world. We must reject and resist every temptation, as Jesus did (Matt 4:1–11), to be a master.

Jesus' teaching on materialism is an inherent part of servanthood. Give to him who asks. Sell your possessions and give alms. If your enemy hungers, feed him. Love your neighbor as yourself. These are not obscure teachings. These represent the ethical heart of the New Testament call to discipleship.

We commonly refer to Matthew 28:19–20 as the "Great Commission." It is not basically a commission to preach, although it is widely interpreted as such. I know of no modern-day evangelist who is carrying out the great commission. For Jesus says that we are to teach all nations all the things that Jesus taught us. And Jesus has principally taught us how to die, how to empty ourselves, how to pick up our cross. There is no gospel, no belief, no abundant life, and no credible proclamation of the word or the kingdom unless the cross is central.

What we find in the modern church is a sort of folk religion of wishful thinking. There is the thought, and it is a commendable one, that those who have been "blessed" ought to do something for the less fortunate. But while I recognize the genuineness of the motivation and the approximate goodness of the result, I do not recognize the relationship to Jesus of Nazareth or his teaching.

There is only one ultimate good—to know Jesus Christ. It is in the act of knowing him that we lose ourselves and our possessions. It is in the act of losing ourselves and our possessions that the world is enriched. This is the sequence that must not be reversed or cut short. In the name of Christ we become poor for the sake of the world. Christianity clearly eclipses the humanitarian ideal, just as the New Testament eclipses the Old. While we ought to have a profound respect for the humanitarian ethic, we ought also to understand that Christ beckons us beyond kindness and liberality to servanthood and poverty.

If we are seriously considering the life of self-denial, two components are absolutely necessary. I believe they deserve special mention, even though they have been indicated already, because they can be easily overlooked.

The first component is joy; the second is love.

If we are going to follow Christ to the cross by the power of the Holy Spirit, then we will experience an increasing joy in our lives in inverse proportion to our decreasing resources. I am struck by the attitudes of two individuals who were discussed earlier. The rich young ruler went away "sorrowful" because he had great possessions. He stands in stark contrast to the man who, discovering the treasure of the kingdom of heaven hidden in a field, "joyfully" goes and sells all that he has and buys that field. The standards of this world are reversed by the values of the kingdom. Which kingdom are we a part of? If our poverty is unattended by joy, then we have reason to question whether it is the poverty mandated by the New Testament. The glum ascetic spirit is not the spirit of Christ.

The emptying process, secondly, must be motivated by love for others if it is to be a spiritually redemptive process. We are not controlled by a sterile mechanization of the dynamic of Christ. Nor are we motivated by guilt. "If I give away all I have . . .," says Paul, "but have not love, I gain nothing" (1 Cor 13:3, RSV). Jesus was not driven by shame when he left the glory of the Father to dwell among us; he rightfully belonged in heaven. But he was drawn by compassion. Love is such a personal and intimate feeling that it causes us to become poor in spirit as well as poor in outward reality. It gives birth to a spirit of partnership and a sharing of lives. This is why I have become more and more suspicious of the mission projects that allow us to give impersonally. Redemptive giving and the essence of discipleship mean that we live with the oppressed and become one with them. Writing out checks for worthy causes is a step in the right direction, and for many it is the first step. Venturing into the congregation of the poor for a day or a summer is a further step. Finally, love will lead us out of the heaven of our secure community and give us the mind of Christ, who for the joy that was set before him endured the cross. This giving of the body, broken for the world, becomes the norm for the Christian. The deepest love and joy issue in this ultimate crucifixion experience, and the cross supplies, in turn, a deeper love and joy.

The sorrow of oppression can never be cancelled out in this life, and we do ourselves a great disservice if we manage to escape the constraints of love. As an unknown poet has written:

If love should count you worthy

And should deign one day to seek your door and be your guest—

Pause ere you draw the bolt and bid him rest, if in your old content you would remain.

For not alone he enters.

In his train are children of the mists, the lonely guest, dreams of the unfulfilled and unpossessed, and sorrow, and lifes immemorial pain.

He wakes desires you never may forget.

He shows you stars you never saw before.

He makes you share with him forevermore the burden of the world's divine regret.

How wise you were to open not.

And yet, how poor, if you should turn him from the door.

It is a hot summer night in the city as I write this message to my friends. Those of you who are familiar with inner city neighborhoods know what heat and humidity bring to the streets: A man sits on his cement stoop watching his portable TV. Drunks stagger out of bars. Old men and women wait for buses or walk alone. Children play on the sidewalk long after dark without supervision. Teenage boys nurse bottles of warm wine. Somehow humanity does not seem to be at its prettiest tonight as the hour approaches eleven. I suppose respectable people are indoors, and perhaps that is why I felt a little uncomfortable when I walked down to the corner a few moments ago. But I am learning to love these people a little bit. I feel sadness more deeply than ever before as I sense the oppressed spirit of humanity.

What can we do together to help? Beneath the anger of much that I say and more that I feel, I want to reach out and say "Jesus is Lord" to these fellow travelers. I know that one option would be to try to remain unmoved and untouched. Another would be to drop my bag of oranges and run. A third, and the one that I have chosen, would be to become continuously involved to the end that I myself might enter the ranks of the oppressed, and might find Jesus there.

But reaching out to the oppressed is not all that I want to do. From the cross Jesus also offers healing to the oppressor. This task is by far the more difficult for me—to reach out in redemptive love to that church that I believe has become an unwitting agent of injustice. Perhaps the reason I hope and believe so firmly that the church will one day be saved is because I find myself still deeply imbued with its complacency. When I reach out to the oppressor, I am really seeking the fullness of my own salvation. And so I yearn for both the master and the slave, the rich and the poor, that each might find the sufficient grace of God.

The following suggestions may be helpful to some who would like guidance in applying biblical principles regarding materialism to their everyday lives. These are not a substitute for the leading of the Holy Spirit. God loves a cheerful giver, motivated by a growing compassion and personal involvement. So these guidelines are not meant to be imposed upon you. They are meant to stimulate your own creativity and to give you some initial direction. They may be considered by individuals or families or church or community groups.

1. Begin to make friends with the poor, and develop an increasing sensitivity to human need through your own involvement with immediate neighbors and through more informed awareness of your neighbors in other parts of the world.

2. Make a list of your own current material needs and a list of the needs of your neighbors as you have come to know them.

Try to consider your own needs through the eyes of a less fortunate person. For example, you may think that you need a new home, and perhaps you do. But you should come to that conclusion only after you have considered the viewpoint of one of your million brothers and sisters who sleep on the streets of Bombay every night.

3. Begin to depend upon God for your daily bread. Convert whatever treasure you may have stored up on earth into readily available cash or goods.

4. Determine what your material resources are for the coming week. Take into account not only your weekly income, but your liquid assets and whatever abundance you may have of clothes, food, furniture, housing, etc.

5. Love your neighbor as yourself by prayerfully applying your resources to the needs of yourself and others. Remember that the others in your widening circle of relationships are representative of Jesus Christ. They have as much claim on your goods as you do.

6. In cases where you are meeting the needs of someone you personally know, be careful not to be paternalistic. You may have to be creative and anonymous in your giving. As you become increasingly one with the poor, you will hopefully have opportunity to receive as well as give. In giving and receiving, the greatest joy comes when we are able to affirm the human dignity of both ourselves and others.

This listing approach seems too mechanical, but it is not meant to be. The sharing of the good news of Christ is a natural spiritual process. But I err on the side of the mechanical for the sake of setting before us some concrete goals and approaches.

I feel like I am with you on this adventure of compassion, and I feel like I am starting from scratch. May God bless us on our journey.

AFTERWORD

I WROTE THESE ESSAYS over forty years ago. Would I have expressed my thoughts differently if I were writing them today? Of course I would. I am a different person now.

I have worked for the past four decades for two different Episcopal churches—All Saints Church, Pasadena, from 1974 to 2002, and the Church of Our Saviour, San Gabriel, from 2002 until the present day. My work has primarily been with the poor, homeless, mentally ill, addicted, and incarcerated, but secondarily I have been a full participant in the liturgical life and the fellowship of these two largely white, upper-middle-class congregations. I straddle two worlds. I have found plenty of opportunities to reach out to my fellow parishioners of privilege in the same way I reach out to the less fortunate. People are lonely; people have health issues; people struggle with addiction, and sometimes incarceration, at both ends of the economic spectrum. I have learned that practicing the presence of God and representing that presence to others is the greatest gift I can bring to anyone, anywhere, in any circumstance. And it is a gift blesses the benefactor more than the beneficiary.

I have come through my own battle with addiction and I have, to date, overcome its cunning, baffling, and powerful interruption of my life and career. I have learned a lot about tolerance, acceptance, and serenity. During my one-month participation at a residential recovery program in Arizona fourteen years ago, I went around with a sign stating "No Sarcasm." Sarcasm is literally a "tearing of the flesh." I had to give up sarcasm to reinforce my own self-worth and to give dignity to others, and to express my love for self and for others without any "buts" or reservations. There are many examples of sarcasm and hyperbole in the text of this book, and I have largely decided to leave them intact. After all, these are "period essays," as Ched Myers correctly points out in his wonderful foreword, and at that time in my life they accurately reflected my thoughts.

(In my defense regarding my use of sarcasm and hyperbole in the past, I want to point out that I am following in the footsteps of three of my mentors: my own earthly father, whose humorous sarcasm was a trademark; the Apostle Paul, whose epistles include sarcastic admonitions to the church; and Jesus of Nazareth, whose stories are replete with examples.)

I have also become, at the age of seventy, a deacon in the Episcopal Church. That means I now am formally charged with bringing the world of the poor to the attention of the church, and the witness of the church to the attention of the poor. It also means that I am officially a member of the clergy, a card-carrying member of the religious establishment. When I get to heaven I am going to have a lot of explaining to do!

I was an evangelical Presbyterian in my formative youth and in all the days leading up to the first publication of these essays in the early 1970s. Now I am an evangelical Episcopalian. That is, I am an Episcopalian who loves the Bible and who loves Jesus. I first read the Bible front to back during the summer between my junior and senior years in high school. I met Jesus for the first time at my infant baptism and then, more knowingly, during that same high school summer at the New Wilmington Missionary Conference. I became an Episcopalian because All Saints was sponsoring a social outreach effort that attracted me to its cause in 1974. I am at Church of Our Saviour because they revived my career and my life post-addiction in 2002.

AFTERWORD

While I disagree with some of the theology and social practices of my evangelical sisters and brothers, I cling to the term "evangelical" because I love the Word and I love the Lord.

This book represents a serious indictment of the church, and a serious challenge to the faithful believer. I stand by that indictment, because it offers the church and the individual Christian a path to relevance and renewal in our 21st-century world.

Beyond being an indictment, it is also a love letter to the church. I desire an expression of the corporate body of Christ that is more in keeping with the mind of Christ. Than is my fervent wish. If I can move myself and a few others toward that glorious goal I will have accomplished my purpose.

www.ingramcontent.com/pod-product-compliance
Lightning Source LLC
Chambersburg PA
CBHW030853090426
42737CB00009B/1219